Norfolk Stories of the Supernatural

Betty Puttick

COUNTRYSIDE BOOKS
NEWBURY, BERKSHIRE

First published 2000

COUNTRYSIDE BOOKS
3 Catherine Road
Newbury, Berkshire

To view our complete range of books,
please visit us at
www.countrysidebooks.co.uk

ISBN 1 85306 649 4

Designed by Graham Whiteman
Cover painting by Colin Doggett

Produced through MRM Associates Ltd., Reading
Printed by J. W. Arrowsmith Ltd., Bristol

Contents

Introduction 7

1. The Heart of King's Lynn 9
2. The Brown Lady of Raynham Hall 15
3. Armine and the Carpet 21
4. Betty of the Bell 25
5. Waterside Mysteries 30
6. The Headless Smuggler 37
7. White Roses from a Ghost 40
8. Timeslips 47
9. The Busiest Ghost in England 53
10. The Lady in the Chair 57
11. The Haunting of 19 Magdalen Street 62
12. The White Ladies of Norfolk 65
13. Haunted Hostelries 70
14. Ghosts that Haunt the Royals 78

15. On the Road 81

16. The Crusaders of Ingham 87

17. Ghostly Bookworms 91

18. The Curious Case of the Egyptian Princess's Mummy 96

19. Will o' the Wisps, Black Dogs and Other Mysteries 102

20. The Maddermarket Ghost 109

21. Bircham Newton 112

22. Ghosts Galore 118

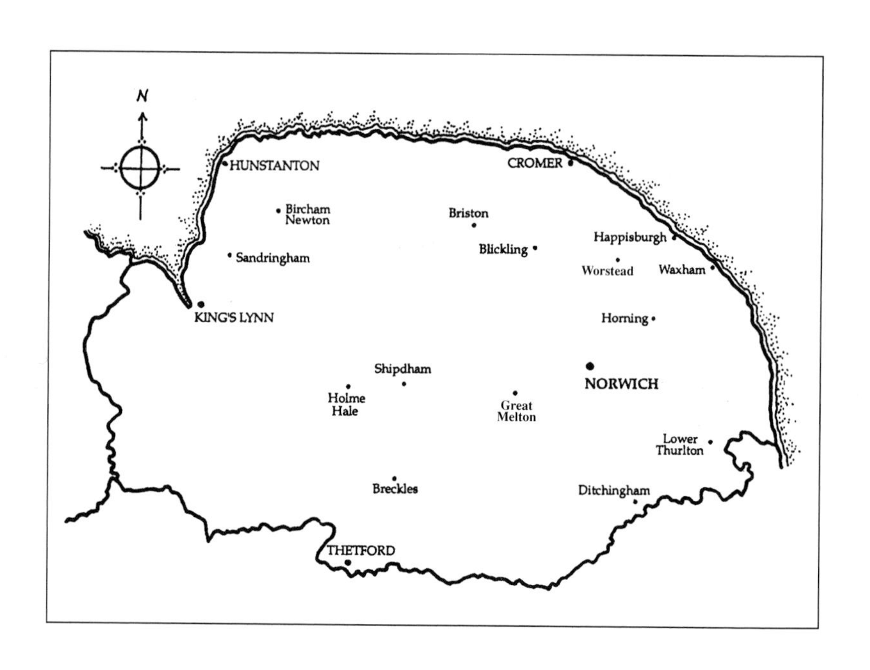

Acknowledgements

My grateful thanks to everyone who took the time and trouble to help me with my enquiries, especially Wesley Downes, Bryan Hall, Tony Broughall, Harold H. Taylor, Keith Webster and Dave Chisnell.

We believe in ghosts in East Anglia – or if we do not admit that we believe in them, we have a hair-raising collection of them.

J. Wentworth Day

Introduction

IF YOU have never visited Norfolk, you probably believe Noel Coward's comment: 'Very flat, Norfolk!' I expect it keeps many people away. But when I explored Norfolk for the first time I found it a well kept secret, and like others who know and love the place I hesitate to share it. Sufficient to say I found long, blissfully empty roads, hedges brimming with wild flowers, shady woodland and green acres stretching for ever, interspersed with sudden stretches of shining blue flax. And, in the summer, poppies everywhere.

And as for ghosts – as J. Wentworth Day said, Norfolk has a hair-raising collection of them. Some of the most famous ghosts of all can be found here such as the Brown Lady of Raynham Hall whose shadowy photograph has adorned countless ghost books. And, of course, Henry VIII's luckless Queen, Anne Boleyn, who sometimes stops off at Blickling Hall, her childhood home, on her eternal round of visits to everywhere she ever lived.

I was lucky enough to meet a number of any ghostwriter's favourite person, the eye witness, and found that even if a vintage ghost has featured in books galore, some of them are still making personal appearances!

There are in Norfolk grand houses where the past seems very close, and white or grey (and brown!) ladies haunt the centuries away, but there are also offices, shops, an airfield and a fire station where revenants from the past walk nonchantly through walls that may not have been there in their time. Longfellow wrote of harmless phantoms with feet that make no sound upon the floor, but many a shadowy wraith is surprisingly heavy footed!

Norfolk has some interesting old inns, many with a 'regular' who never goes home, and the Broads and the old fenland areas are a treasure trove of mysterious and colourful tales. And there are stranger stories still . . . I hope you will enjoy them all as you read on.

Betty Puttick

1

The Heart of King's Lynn

KING'S LYNN'S Tuesday Market Place is a lively, busy place with a gruesome history and more than a few tales of the supernatural. On one side of the square you can find No 15/16, a handsome building now used as offices, and above a central window over the doorway is a small carving of a diamond within which is a heart, a symbol with a tragic story.

In harsher days Tuesday Market Place saw the cruel end of several women, some accused of witchcraft, others of murder, who met their death by hanging, burning or, in one dreadful case, by boiling alive. This victim was Margaret Day, a maidservant found guilty of poisoning her mistress and other members of the family in 1531, and since Henry VIII had decreed this method of execution for anyone convicted of murder by poisoning, this was Margaret Day's terrifying fate.

Before a great crowd in the market place she was suspended above a giant cauldron over a huge fire and when the water came to the boil, she was lowered down into it, then raised and lowered again until she died. Legend has it that at that moment her heart burst from her body to hit the wall of the house where the heart carving now marks the spot.

But this is only one version of how the heart design came to be there. Mary Smith was burnt as a witch in 1616. She was the wife of a glovemaker in King's Lynn, who admitted that the Devil in the form of a black man had given her the power over others that was to be her downfall. Various people who fell foul of Mary were cursed by her to unfortunate effect and her pleas that the Devil had forced her to do it were of no avail. She spent the night before her execution at the Gryphyn inn, now superseded by the Duke's Head Hotel, where she prayed for forgiveness, and went to her death with amazing calmness. Impressed by her demeanour, the crowd sang psalms as the faggots were lighted, and in her case too, legend has it that as she died, her heart leapt out towards the place now marked by the famous heart carving.

Yet another version of Mary Smith's story says that her prosecutor was the Rev Alexander Roberts, known as 'The Preacher of God's Word', who published *A Treatise of Witchcraft* but Mary protested her innocence and predicted that when she died her heart would fly forth and perch above the window of the magistrate who had condemned her.

But there is yet another candidate. Margaret Read, known locally as Shady Meg, lived in a poky, rundown little house down by the river Ouse, and locals were fearful of her reputation. For strange things happened around Shady Meg, and she was reputed to have inherited her power from her aunt, Agnes, known to have been a dabbler in the black arts.

Various people visited Shady Meg's insalubrious dwelling for purposes of their own, including one young woman who had borne a child out of wedlock and had been deserted by the father, one Nick Kirk. The local gossips shook their heads as Nick laughed defiantly when he heard that his former lover, bent on vengeance, was seen to visit Shady Meg, but in no time he fell ill with severe chest and stomach pains, and three days later he was dead!

His parents reported Meg to the authorities, and when her cottage was searched they found incriminating evidence – a small male figure with pins stuck into its chest and stomach!

The well-known method of testing a witch, known as 'swimming', was used on Shady Meg. With her hands and feet bound together, she was thrown into the river Ouse with a long rope tied round her neck. She floated at first, then screaming curses, she sank under the water. After a time she was hauled out, spluttering and choking, but alive, which according to the beliefs of the time meant she was a witch.

On the morning of 20th July 1590, Margaret Read was burnt at the stake in Tuesday Market Place, and as the flames hid her from view, suddenly with a bang something was seen to fly out and strike the nearby wall!

So whose heart was it that struck the wall of No 15/16 at Lynn's Tuesday Market Place? It is a strange and bizarre story and while the heart design remains on the wall, the legend and speculation will, no doubt, remain.

With such a history, it would not be surprising to find some ghosts lingering in the area, and the Duke's Head Hotel can claim a few hauntings. Instead of the usual white or grey ladies, this hotel has a Red Lady, so called because she patrols the staircases and corridors in a scarlet gown. It's said the strain of choosing between her two lovers was too much for her, and so she hanged herself!

Another suicide is believed to haunt Room 18. This was a young sprig of the aristocracy who, around the end of the 18th century, was in such trouble over his gambling debts that he shot himself. He was found, seriously wounded, outside in the market place, and was brought into the inn and taken to his room, No 18. A doctor was called, but the young man was beyond his help, and he died with the words 'I shall return'.

The commercial travellers and other gentlemen who frequented the Duke's Head were uneasy about Room 18, which was often left unused when the inn was otherwise full. One old regular liked to use either Room 17 or Room 19, so that he could store his goods in Room 18, but on one occasion he recorded an alarming experience.

He had been asleep but something woke him and he heard what sounded like moaning coming from the next room – No 18! He knew it was unoccupied, and when the moans continued he got up and cautiously opened his bedroom door.

'As I did so a tall figure in white glided along the passage until it seemed to disappear in the sitting room at the end of it. I went to this room and searched it thoroughly, but not a vestige of what I had seen could I find, and I returned to my room quite unnerved. I shall prefer to sleep in another part of the house next time I come,' he said.

Another inn in the Tuesday Market Place area is the Globe which at times has an unpleasant chill in the air and the feeling of a watchful presence which has made staff feel nervous. It has even been used for sponsored 'spook-watches' in aid of charity.

The trouble seemed to start in the 1960s when the old

stables were converted into a dining room. In her book *Ghosts and Legends of King's Lynn*, Alison Gifford says that older Lynn residents remembered that when they were children it was said that there had once been a dreadful fight to the death between two men in the stables. What was it all about? The details were lost in the mists of memory.

But during her research, Alison Gifford discovered an interesting old photograph which had been reproduced in the *Lynn News and Advertiser* for 1933. It shows a group of the kitchen and yard staff of the Globe taken some time around the late 19th century, judging by the Victorian clothes, and includes Philip Smith (yardman), called The Boxer, and states, 'Philip Smith died after a fight in the stables with another man'.

Mr Smith appears to have been a tall, well-built man, but there is no clue to his assailant or the reason they fought. Was it over some pretty serving maid perhaps? There is only one woman in the photograph, simply described as 'cook', and she looks more of a Mrs Bridges than a heart-breaker. There they stand, frozen in time in the inn yard, complete with a rather bored looking horse. What passionate emotions were hidden behind those unsmiling faces. Was one of them to be Philip Smith's killer? And is the man they called The Boxer still lingering where once the stables stood, the reason for that unnatural chill?

Finally a footnote to life at the Duke's Head long ago. John Green was sacked from his job there and set up as the tavern shoe black, but through heavy drinking and gambling he got into serious debt, so decided to sell his wife! He placed a halter round her neck and led her to the market place where he invited bids. One's heart bleeds for Mrs Green, as there was no rush to acquire her, and the only offer her husband received was a gallon of beer which, says the report, 'he readily accepted'.

2

The Brown Lady of Raynham Hall

IN THE realm of stately home hauntings the Brown Lady of Raynham Hall is rightly one of the most famous with a host of dramatic sightings since her death in 1726.

She is believed to be Dorothy Walpole, sister of Britain's first Prime Minister, Robert Walpole of Houghton Hall, and although those who have encountered her ghost describe its appearance as frightening and even 'malevolent', in life she was a beautiful and charming woman, but whose fondness for pretty clothes verged on the extravagant. This may have led to her serious differences with her husband, the 2nd Marquess Townshend, known as 'Turnip' Townshend, who introduced the vegetable to England and revolutionised crop rotation.

There are different versions of Dorothy's story. Her father was made guardian of Charles Townshend, then 13 years old, and when in due course Dorothy was 15, and Charles 12 years older, he fell deeply in love and wanted to marry her. But Dorothy's father refused to allow it, as he thought he would be accused of having his eye on the Townshend fortune and property.

One version of the story says Dorothy did not share Charles's feelings, in fact she found him repulsive. But the more romantic version has her plunging into a frivolous life of parties and scandalous behaviour to forget her broken heart, ultimately becoming the mistress of a well-known roué, Lord Wharton.

Meanwhile, Charles Townshend had married, but his wife died in 1713, and he and Dorothy were united at last. There seems little doubt that after a time the marriage was unhappy, and whatever caused Charles's change of heart towards her, he deprived Dorothy of the care of her children who were put in charge of his mother. Miserable without them and unkindly treated by her husband, Dorothy is said to have been confined to her rooms, and within a short time died at the age of 40.

One tradition says that Dorothy was starved to death, and another that she fell, or was pushed, down the grand staircase and was killed. But the contemporary announcement of her death, on 29th March 1726, gives the cause as smallpox.

Many hauntings have a tragic background, and whatever the truth about the manner of Dolly Townshend's death, she did not rest in peace and her ghost was soon seen by servants, family and visitors.

One important visitor was George IV, when Prince Regent, who was, of course, put in the State Bedroom with unfortunate results. He roused the whole household, reporting furiously that he had been disturbed by 'a little lady all dressed in brown, with dishevelled hair and a face of ashy paleness' who stood by his bedside. 'I will not pass another hour in this accursed house,' cried his Highness, 'for I have seen that what I hope to God I may never see again.'

The Brown Lady's sighting in 1849 was reported in *Rifts in the Veil* by Lucia Stone, a member of a large houseparty at Raynham. Major Loftus, a relative of the hosts Lord and Lady Charles Townshend, had stayed up late with another guest playing chess, and as they went up to bed, his attention was called to a lady in a brown dress standing on the landing. He did not recognise her as one of the guests, but when he went to speak to her, she vanished.

Determined to waylay the mysterious lady, he waited up the following night, and managed to come face to face with her. In the light of his lamp he could see her clearly and described her wearing a richly brocaded brown dress with a coif on her head, but to his horror, instead of eyes she had two dark, hollow sockets. He made a sketch of what he had seen and showed it next morning to the other guests, which inspired some of them to do some ghost-hunting on their own account, but the Brown Lady was not tempted to make another appearance.

But the effect on the servants was unfortunate; the entire staff gave notice and left! Although Lord Charles declared that he had seen the family ghost several times, he was suspicious that this time some annoying practical joker might be responsible, and in lieu of the missing staff, he brought in a number of police, but no trickster or the Brown Lady herself rewarded their vigil.

The ghost received an unexpected reception when Captain Marryat, the famous author of *Mr Midshipman Easy*, was staying at Raynham Hall. The Captain briskly dismissed the notion of ghosts and insisted on sleeping in the haunted bedroom, which contained a portrait of the Brown Lady. A lesser man might have felt uneasy as in the flickering candlelight the eyes in the picture appeared unnaturally alive, and the expression on the face seemed the embodiment of evil. But not Marryat; he was getting ready for bed when two other guests arrived at his room to ask his advice about a gun for the shooting party next day.

Captain Marryat went to their room to see the gun and was returning along the shadowy corridor when he saw a woman coming towards him. Her feet made no sound, and the lamp she was holding illuminated a figure unmistakably the image of the portrait in his room. According to Marryat, the apparition looked at him 'in such a diabolical manner' that even he was frightened and, gun in hand, he fired point-blank, full in her face. The bullets went straight through her and lodged in the door behind, and the figure vanished.

It's said that the brave Captain slept with his loaded pistols under his pillow for the rest of his visit.

Gwladys, Marchioness Townshend, in *True Ghost Stories* (1936), says that her son George and a friend, when they were small boys, met a lady on the staircase, who frightened and puzzled them because they could see the stairs through her!

And in the 1920s Sir Henry ('Tim') Birkin sat up one night hoping to encounter the Brown Lady, but although he waited in vain, his dog showed signs of acute terror in the small hours.

Marchioness Townshend also mentions other spectres at Raynham such as two ghost children, a phantom spaniel whose paws patter on the staircase although he is not seen, and the charming Red Cavalier. This is the Duke of Monmouth, Charles II's ill-fated son, who once stayed at Raynham Hall with his royal father. He haunts the bedroom he once used, now known as the Monmouth Room, and the Marchioness tells the story of a lovely 'deb of the year' who insisted on sleeping there, hoping for a visit from the notorious charmer.

But despite the Duke's well-known eye for a pretty woman, she was unlucky. The next occupant of the room a few days later was a 'spinster of uncertain age' who, according to her hostess, was sadly destined to live a drab life devoid of romance. However, she woke that night to find the dashing Red Cavalier standing at the end of her bed, 'smiling in a most encouraging manner'. As he went he gave her a charming courtly bow and faded away through the wall, leaving her with a cherished memory of her glamorous visitor.

The famous photograph of the Brown Lady has been frequently reproduced in books about ghosts and hauntings. It happened in the thirties that two photographers from *Country Life* magazine were taking a series of photographs of Raynham Hall. Captain Provand was photographing the staircase when his assistant, Indra Shira, suddenly noticed a misty figure approaching down the stairs. He quickly urged Captain Provand to take an exposure, which he did, although he himself had seen nothing. He protested that Indra Shira must have imagined it, and declared that even if there was something there, nothing would appear when the negative was developed.

But Indra Shira insisted he had seen a figure so ethereal that the steps were visible through it, and later when they were developing the negatives the Captain could see that there was definitely something on the staircase negative. Indra Shira hurried downstairs to the chemist below their studio and brought Benjamin Jones back to be a witness that the negative had not been tampered with. Later a number of experts examined it and were satisfied that the picture had not been faked in any way.

There seems no doubt that Raynham Hall is haunted by echoes of its past. In *True Ghost Stories* the Marchioness Townshend said that at times the sound of whispers and the swish of silken skirts testify 'that the picture gallery is alive with the "Quality" who ruffled it in the days when the splendour of the Great House was undiminished'. And sometimes in one room the heavy chairs which are usually set against the walls are found in the morning companionably grouped around a large card table! Are the Brown Lady and the Red Cavalier among the players I wonder?

3

Armine and the Carpet

THIS IS the story of one woman's obsession – an emotion so powerful that it brought her back in spirit long after her death. It was neither a place or a person which meant so much to Armine le Strange, but a carpet! But not just any carpet, it was an antique carpet of great beauty given to her by the Shah of Persia and so dearly cherished by the recipient that her last dying thoughts were for its safety.

Hunstanton Hall has been the ancestral home of the le Strange family for hundreds of years, but the once splendid Tudor manor house was devastated by fire in 1853 when valuable old furniture and pictures were destroyed, followed by another fire in 1951.

But these disasters were in the future when Armine, widowed after the death of her husband Henry Styleman, inherited Hunstanton Hall on the death of her brother in 1760. Her portrait shows a woman whose dark eyes seem uncomfortably alive and her expression suggests a strong, determined character in spite of her apparent age.

But during her time at Hunstanton Hall Armine needed all the strength of character she could muster thanks to the overwhelming problems created by her eldest son, Nicholas, known throughout Norfolk as 'The Jolly Gentleman'.

'Jolly' Nicholas certainly was, but also selfish, pleasure loving and a compulsive gambler, and it was to satisfy his endless succession of gambling debts that the many treasures of Hunstanton Hall gradually disappeared, to the rage and distress of his mother. Books from the splendid library, valuable plate and jewellery which had adorned the le Strange ladies for generations, all vanished into the black hole of Nicholas's gambling debts.

As one after the other precious possessions were sold, Armine naturally thought that her son's eye would sooner or later fall upon the carpet she valued so much. In 1768 she became ill, and knowing that she was close to death, she asked him to come to see her.

'You have sold nearly everything,' she accused him, 'and I am told that if I were able to look out of the window of my bedchamber, I should miss the deer in the Park.'

Quite unabashed, Nicholas cheerfully admitted that he had lost them at play the previous week. Armine voiced her fears that once she was dead, he would also dispose of her precious carpet, which was of considerable value. Nicholas appeared shocked at such an idea, and protested that he had never even considered it. But Armine knew him better than that, and with all the force she could muster, demanded his solemn promise that he would never sell the carpet.

Nicholas clasped his mother's hand in his, and fervently promised to do as she asked.

'Remember, Nicholas,' she continued, 'if you break your promise, or if you or anyone else commit the enormity of selling the carpet, or letting it go out of the Hall, I shall return and haunt this house. I swear it, and I know I shall be permitted to do so.'

Even Nicholas was impressed by his dying mother's words, and after her death, he decided to avoid temptation by having the carpet taken up from the drawing room, and stored away in a wooden box, well nailed down. And there for the rest of Nicholas's lifetime, and beyond, Armine's beloved carpet mouldered away in some dusty store room in the Hall, undisturbed and forgotten.

Eighty years later the Hall passed into the possession of Hamon le Strange who married Emmeline Austin from Boston, known as the American Beauty, who was obviously as lively and energetic as she was beautiful. Delighted to be the mistress of an English stately home, Emmeline set about exploring it, finding interesting areas obviously forgotten and untouched for years. The discovery of an ancient box was quite exciting for her, but once opened, the dusty old carpet she found was not quite the treasure she anticipated. Nevertheless, instead of putting it back where she found it, Emmeline decided that it could be divided up into useful hearthrugs for poor members of the locality.

Full of benevolence she set off in her carriage with her pile of rugs which she presented to cottage families, and returned home well satisfied with her generosity. But as her carriage arrived at the gatehouse, she was alarmed to find that she was being watched from the window by an elderly woman whose face expressed anger and hatred. With a sense of shock she recognised Armine le Strange whose portrait hung in the Hall. Emmeline hurried in to tell her husband of her frightening encounter with the ghost of his ancestor, and remembering the story of

Armine's threat to haunt the Hall if ever her beloved carpet was disposed of, Hamon le Strange told his wife that her hearthrugs must be recovered and returned to the box forthwith.

Realising how embarrassing this would be, Emmeline at first refused. Perhaps she tried to convince herself that she had imagined that disturbing sighting of Armine, but within hours she knew it had been no hallucination. For several nights the Hall was haunted by Armine le Strange's restless ghost to the sheer terror of the household, and Emmeline was obliged to take action. The recipients of her previous generosity were no doubt delighted to receive good quality Axminster rugs instead, and the pieces of the Shah's carpet were reunited, and safely stowed away once more.

However, unfortunately the haunting of Hunstanton Hall by Armine le Strange was not so easily terminated. Her ghost has continued to appear from time to time, possibly still resentful that although she managed to prevent her wayward son Nicholas turning her beloved carpet into ready cash, the innocent desire of a pretty American wife to do a little good in the village was almost as destructive.

4

Betty of the Bell

THE BELL is an old coaching inn with a long and interesting history which has stood on the corner of King Street and Bridge Street, Thetford for centuries, in fact there is a record of it dating back to 1493, and it has a long and interesting history.

Its heyday was in the late 18th century when Thetford had its own racecourse, and the then landlord, Richard Hovell, was Clerk of the Course. In those exciting days the inn was thronged with visitors enjoying its famous hospitality.

The Bell had a number of notable landlords over the years, but one name has never been forgotten, that of the landlady Betty Radcliffe, who must have been there in the 19th century as she is remembered in the memoirs of Lord Albemarle, published in 1876. He recalled, 'When the Duke of York changed horses at the Bell he always had a talk with Betty. As he was paying her one morning for the horses, she jingled the money in her hand and said to his Royal Highness, "I may as well take a little of your money, for I have been paying your father's taxes for many a long day." '

Obviously she was a lady of character, and also reputed

to be quite a beauty. But Betty's story is a sad one, whichever version you hear, as both end in tragedy which apparently keeps her restless spirit still earthbound after more than a century.

It seems that Betty had a love affair with an ostler at the inn, but passion eventually cooled on one side or the other. One version of the story says that when Betty had wanted to end their relationship, in a fit of jealous rage the ostler murdered her. The other version has it that Betty's lover heartlessly jilted her, and she committed suicide by throwing herself from a balcony down to the cobblestones below.

Either way, this was not the end of the Bell's famous landlady. As a member of staff said to me when I had lunch there in 1999, 'She's still around!'

In her lifetime Betty Radcliffe preferred to live in what is called The Ancient House in White Hart Street, now a museum, but it is in Room 12 at the Bell that she is reputed to linger. This is said to have been the room where Betty's ostler used to sleep, and where the lovers kept their assignations. Several people have claimed to have experienced odd happenings and uncomfortable feelings there.

It is well known that building work often seems to promote supernatural activity, and in 1964 when considerable alterations were taking place at the Bell, the then landlord and his wife had to change bedrooms several times while electrical and plumbing work was in progress.

Usually their dog Janey slept quite peacefully in her basket in whichever bedroom they used, but when they had to move to No 12, it was a different matter. Nothing would persuade the dog to settle down there, she stayed outside the door whining miserably all night, which reminded the landlord and his wife that dogs are supposed to be able to sense a supernatural presence, and although previously sceptical, they wondered if perhaps there might be something in the stories after all!

Some of these concern a 17th century mural above the fireplace in the haunted bedroom; this is protected by a sheet of glass which fits close to the painting, which makes it all the more odd that sometimes fingermarks have been found on the inside of the glass. In March 1992 a newly married couple, Colin and Maureen Mitchell, arrived to spend a few days of their honeymoon at the Bell. They were delighted with their beautiful room with its ancient timbers and four poster bed, and the interesting old mural on the wall behind its glass case. During the night Colin woke, hearing footsteps outside their room, but thought little of it until he realised that the footsteps were now inside the room. He tried to think of a rational explanation, such as the creaking as the old floorboards expanded, but then he could see an orange glow which appeared in front of the mural. He told himself this must be caused by the traffic lights in the street outside reflecting in the glass of the mural, but he was suddenly aware that the temperature in the room had become icy cold, and in his words 'there was a young girl standing in the middle of the room. She looked about 14 and was wearing a white short sleeved dress that came down to her ankles, with a sash round her waist and a garland of blue and white flowers round her blonde hair. Her face was completely expressionless, and she walked straight across to the window as if she was unaware of the furniture, and as she got to the window she disappeared.'

Colin realised with a shock that he was seeing a ghost, and in panic, he turned to wake Maureen, but then felt the sheets being lifted up over his head with the sensation that someone was tucking him in!

He must have dozed off after that, but in the morning when he remembered the strange events of the night he looked at the mural, and found a small handprint on the inside of the glass.

The couple spoke to the manager about what had happened, and he told them that other guests staying in their room, and the one next to it, had had similar experiences. Even so Colin and Maureen decided to stay on, and on the second night both woke to see the same orange glow on the mural, but this time, there was no reappearance of the ghost. Yet once again, next morning they found a second handprint inside the glass of the mural.

A different manager was on duty and when they told him what had happened he showed them a portrait over the lounge mantelpiece.

'This is Betty Radcliffe,' he said, 'she used to own the hotel'. Colin was shaken by this information as he realised that the ghostly girl he had seen resembled the same woman, at a younger age.

That evening as Colin was watching television, the handle of the wardrobe door started tapping and there was interference on the TV screen. And that night, their last at the Bell, he was woken yet again by the sound of footsteps, and when he opened his eyes he saw the girl in white was sitting on the end of the bed looking at him. Then she got up and moved towards the window, and vanished.

Many other guests have reported similar experiences over the years and the staff are, of course, aware of the happenings. One day two members of staff had just finished cleaning the haunted room and as they left one teasingly said, 'Now Betty, don't go frightening any more of our customers'. Immediately both women felt chilled by a sensation of such intense icy coldness they couldn't wait to get away.

Throughout the country, the number of inns which claim to be haunted is legion. It is hardly surprising as many have been at the centre of local life for centuries with a steady stream of customers including highwaymen, smugglers, soldiers, priests, monks, and even eloping lovers, many contributing their romantic or tragic story to add colour to the hostelry's history. And sometimes perhaps, a sad little ghost like poor Betty Radcliffe.

5

Waterside Mysteries

Wroxham's Roman Visitors

LESS THAN a hundred years ago the Norfolk Broadland area was an isolated and little known place. Today it is a magnet in summertime for holidaymakers drawn by the beauty of the Broads, and many make for Wroxham, one of the busiest and liveliest spots on the river Bure.

Maybe you have whiled away a warm summer afternoon on a pleasant trip downriver in that popular area, with nothing to disturb the peace apart from the chatter of your fellow tourists. And yet there are some strange stories told of this place, of the curious phenomena witnessed at times by visitors over the centuries, and all remarkably similar in detail.

It was on 21st July 1829 that Lord Percival Durand anchored his yacht, the *Amarylis*, in the river Bure, and he and his friends were relaxing on the bank when a rather ragged, odd looking old man came up to them and told them that they were trespassing on crown land. In letters to his father Lord Percival described what happened next.

He and his friends were surprised to be told that they had no right to be there, and asked to whom it belonged.

'To the crown,' they were told. 'To Caesar, his Majesty the Emperor Marcus Aurelius Carausius of the Western Empire.'

It seemed obvious to Lord Percival that the old man was deranged, but he pressed him to tell them who he was.

'I am the Custos Rotulorum for the whole of this part of Britain, and my name is Flavius Mantus,' was the reply.

Lord Percival pointed out that the Roman Empire relinquished these islands fifteen hundred years ago, but the old man would have none of it. 'The Empire continues here today as of old, and I am still the Custos here,' he said. 'Have you come to see the celebrations?'

Telling them that it was the Emperor's birthday, the old man pointed his stick to where the great festival was to take place. And as his listeners glanced back curiously at their strange companion they were astounded to see that he was no longer a shabby, dishevelled old man, but a splendidly garbed Roman officer. And in place of the waters of the broad there was now a huge stone wall enclosing a magnificent Roman amphitheatre decked with colourful banners, which was rapidly filling with people in Roman dress arriving from every direction.

As Lord Percival and his friends took in the scene in stunned astonishment, the noise from the amphitheatre swelled to an excited roar as the people rose to their feet, and a trumpet fanfare greeted the arrival of a huge procession of Roman soldiers followed by a golden chariot drawn by white horses, bearing a Roman general accompanied by full grown lions on golden chains held by warriors, and after them, a procession of prisoners.

At this point the amazing vision faded, and the bedraggled figure of the old man who had first accosted Lord Percival and his friends was seen wandering off to disappear into the woodland.

If this detailed description had been the only record of such a remarkable happening, one might be tempted to think Lord Percival had dozed off on that warm summer afternoon and dreamed the whole thing. But there have been several similar accounts over the years.

In the *Gentlemen's Gazette* of 16th April 1709, the Reverend Thomas Josiah Penston from Durham described his own experience in the same area in the previous March.

He and his family were also on the bank of the Broad enjoying a picnic when they too were accosted by a 'very undesirable looking person' who ordered them away. Annoyed by his manner, they got up to leave but had to move aside quickly to get out of the way of a long procession. Here again before their amazed eyes came the golden chariot containing a 'hideous looking' Roman general, drawn by white stallions and accompanied by lions on chains led by Roman soldiers, with drums and trumpets making a great noise. Hundreds of ragged, long-haired men chained together came after, followed by horsemen and soldiers.

'They passed quite close to us, but no one apparently saw us,' said the Rev Penston, remarking that the noise of their passing was very loud and unmistakable. 'Whither they went or from whence they came I know not, yet they vanished at the lake side.'

Even further back in time, the *Archives of the North-folk* for 1603 describes the strange adventure of Benjamin Curtiss, when he and two friends were bathing in the Great Broad of Wroxham.

They were swimming across from one bank to the other

when to their surprise they could feel their feet touch bottom. They knew that at this point the water was twelve or fourteen feet deep, but suddenly the water had vanished and they found themselves standing in a large arena surrounded by seating, and they themselves dressed as Roman soldiers.

As described by Lord Percival Durand, they saw many coloured flags and banners waving in the breeze around the arena, and they, too, witnessed a huge procession 'many myles longe', and heard the sound of many trumpets.

With remarkable sangfroid, as the amazing sight disappeared the men continued their swim, but on the bank they took it in turns to describe what they had seen and it was obvious that they had all had exactly the same experience.

Charles Sampson who collected these and many other strange ghost stories of the Broads says that this apparition is said to occur between the Ides of March and the Nones of October, notably on the 13th and 16th April, 7th and 21st May, 1st, 4th and 11th June, once in July (no date given), 5th, 13th and 19th August, 13th, 15th, 22nd and 26th September, and 7th and 9th October. Obviously the whole incredible spectacle is only seen on occasion and who can say why it happens at such times and to certain people, but at other times psychically sensitive people on the bank or on the river have seen nothing, but have heard inexplicable sounds like the distant cheering of a multitude of people.

Dead of Night in Fenland

If you visit East Dereham you will see an interesting sign bridging the road leading to the market place. It shows a nun and two deer and a huntsman and his dogs and commemorates a time of famine when in response to the prayers of St Withburga two deer came daily to provide milk for her nunnery. A huntsman set his dogs on the deer but retribution overtook him and he fell from his horse and was killed.

St Withburga was the daughter of Anna, King of the East Angles, who founded a nunnery at East Dereham and, after her death, such was her saintly reputation that people came from far and wide to visit her shrine hoping to be cured of their illnesses and troubles.

When the monks of Ely were in severe financial trouble they had the reprehensible idea of stealing the body of St Withburga so that they could benefit from the pilgrims that flocked to her shrine. And so, at dead of night, they went to Dereham and stole the nun's body which they took by road to Brandon, and then by boat to Ely where she was buried in the cathedral beside the body of her sister, St Etheldreda.

However, although the nuns of Dereham had lost their saint, a well miraculously sprang up at the site of her grave, and continued to be revered as a healing well and place of pilgrimage. The well can still be seen in the churchyard of St Nicholas's church which occupies the site of St Withburga's nunnery.

W.H. Barrett, who, as a boy, heard many tales that had been handed down during the centuries from one old storyteller to another, saved for future generations a wonderful heritage of legends and memories of ghosts, witches and old Fenland characters in his *Tales from the Fens* and *More Tales from the Fens.* He tells a story he had from an eye witness who was fishing one night on the

Little Ouse river, when he noticed a large boat coming down river from the direction of Brandon. It was an unusual boat, and the four men rowing and those on deck were unusual too, as they all wore long hooded cloaks. On the deck was a coffin surrounded by large candles, and one of the men was swinging a censer from which came smoke and 'a queer smell', presumably incense.

The watcher noticed that there wasn't a sound or a ripple on the water as the strange craft went by, and then a weird dirge-like singing began which brought him out in a cold sweat of fear. He watched the boat which remained visible until it was quite out of sight as the water all round it was shining like silver.

Apparently there have been other sightings of what is believed to be a re-enactment of the night the monks from Ely stole St Withburga's body, and Mr Barrett's informant was told that someone from Brandon had actually seen the spectral monks carry the coffin down the road and put it on a boat.

As in the previous story of the Roman amphitheatre, it seems that not every one sees the psychic replay in its entirety or from the same viewpoint. For some there is the whole amazing scene, for others a smaller excerpt, and for others still, just the merest sound echoing down the centuries.

Over the Ice at Hickling Broad

Hickling Broad has a romantic but sad ghost story of young love which ended in tragedy. Lilian Ducker was a pretty young girl, the oldest of the five children of Jesse Ducker of Potter Heigham. And one cold February day when she was out in the village her eye was attracted by a splendidly uniformed young Grenadier home on leave. John Sadler too, had noticed Lilian, and both realised to their delight that they knew each other. They had been childhood friends years ago, and now as they talked together their pleasure at this unexpected meeting turned to love.

They arranged to meet at Swim Coots, on the edge of Hickling Broad, on the Potter Heigham side, near to Lilian's home. But Lilian's father Jesse soon heard about his daughter's romance, and swore that his daughter should never marry a soldier. John told him that once a great battle he was to fight in was over, he would leave the army and be free to settle down.

There was about a week of John's leave left and every evening he skated across Hickling Broad to where Lilian was waiting, her heart beating with love as she heard the sound of his drum and his merry whistle. On the night of 24th February 1814, Lilian was there as dusk fell, and she soon heard the roll of John's drum as he whistled over the ice towards her. But suddenly there was an ominous cracking of the ice and a splash, then a dreadful silence. Lilian screamed. She knew at once what had happened. As John skated towards her he had struck a patch of ice which had given way beneath him.

Heartbroken and desolate, Lilian would never again meet her lover beside Hickling Broad. But it was not the last that Hickling Broad saw of John Sadler. Around February, just as the light is fading, a phantom skater has been seen skimming over the ice towards Potter Heigham. Listen, and some say you may hear a roll on his drum, and others say that as he glides by to the rendezvous he will never keep, he whistles still!

6

The Headless Smuggler

IN HAPPISBURGH in the 18th century people out late at night kept a wary eye open for a particularly gruesome ghost sometimes seen coming from the direction of Cart Gap towards the village street. It appeared to be legless, and at first sight headless, but anyone who nervously glanced back at the retreating figure could see that the head hung down behind, attached to a strip of skin, and a long pigtail almost reached the ground. The figure was dressed in the style of a seafaring man with a wide leather belt fastened by a brass buckle into which was thrust a business-like pistol. A couple of local farmers, braver than the rest, decided to watch for the ghost and one night when it appeared they followed nervously behind and saw it pause by a well, and after throwing the bundle it was carrying down into the depths, it too vanished.

When they told their friends what had happened it was decided to investigate, and a party of locals set off for the well, equipped with a ladder, plenty of rope and a brave volunteer. Taking no chances they at first let down a candle fixed into a ball of clay to test the atmosphere, but everything seemed to be all right so a young man safely seated in a loop of rope was lowered into the well.

Holding a lantern aloft he was slowly dropped a good forty feet down, then he suddenly spotted a piece of blue cloth caught on the side. After showing this to the others he was let down again equipped with a clothes prop, and after a while he called up to say he could feel something at the bottom of the well. Using a pot hook he managed to get hold of it and it was duly hauled up and turned out to be a sack containing a gruesome sight – a pair of boots complete with legs! It was decided that someone should go down the well again to see what else might be there, but the young man was, not surprisingly, somewhat shaken by his ordeal and refused to repeat the experience.

However, after a good swig or two of rum someone else was persuaded to let himself be dropped over the side to see if there was anything else to fish up. He could soon feel something at the bottom of the well but it proved very difficult to hook up and required more rum before he was successful and eventually he was hauled up with a large soggy object. He dropped it on to the ground and when the others crowded round they gasped in horror to see the rotting body of a man. The head attached at the back by just a strip of skin, the clothes, the leather belt and even the pistol told their story. There was no doubt that this was the earthly remains of the ghost.

A little detective work at Cart Gap revealed a large patch of blood, a few coins trampled into the earth and some liquor bottles, and in a broken down old shed they found a pistol, the twin of the one in the murdered man's belt. Smuggling was rife in the area at the time, and the theory locally was that a group of drunken freeloaders had quarrelled over their spoils and one had been murdered by the others.

The story was told in E.R. Suffling's *History and Legends of the Broads District.* The unfortunate victim was never identified and neither were his murderers. The place where the body was found was known as Well Corner, along Whimpwell Street which had a reputation for being haunted as at times it was said that frightening groans were heard coming from the well before a storm, but after a pump was installed the groaning stopped. Later when the pump was no longer used it was some time before it was removed as local people believed that if the pump went the Pump Hill Ghost would start groaning again!

7

White Roses from a Ghost

WHEN I went in search of supernatural Norfolk I soon realised that many of the stories of ghosts and mysteries that I found there were quite unusual, but this story in particular seems unique in my experience.

The details of what happened to a lady called Mrs Goodeve in October 1893 are contained in a booklet called *The Snettisham Ghost* by the Rev Rowland W. Maitland, published by the Psychic Press but when I visited the small Torc bookshop in Snettisham hoping to find a copy, the proprietor told me that she had bought up all the remaining copies and sold the last one twenty years ago. However, luckily I found a copy in Norwich Reference Library and was able to read the extraordinary story which the Rev Maitland pieced together mostly from a report written by Andrew Lang for the Society of Psychical Research, plus Mrs Goodeve's own account.

As the Rev Maitland says, the story is so bizarre that it resembles a fictional gothic romance of the more sensational kind, and yet due to verifiable facts, it appears to be completely genuine.

The story begins in Kent, at 5 Rodney Place, Clifton, where a Mrs Seagrim died on 22nd December 1878. The house was occupied on and off until 1888 when the Ackland family moved in, and they noticed heavy footsteps on the stairs at times, when no one was there, also out of nowhere sometimes water was inexplicably splashed at members of the family when no one else was anywhere near.

Mrs Goodeve, a friend of the Acklands, came on a visit from her London home in October 1893 and also heard the footsteps and night-time sounds as if someone was dragging a heavy weight on the stairs. On the night of 8th/9th October she woke up feeling a cold wind blowing on her face, although the door and windows were closed, and found a ghostly figure, a female, leaning over her. She had a thin, emaciated face but with a kind expression, her head swathed in an Indian shawl.

She spoke to Mrs Goodeve, quite clearly saying 'Follow me'. Mrs Goodeve, obviously a lady of strong nerves, got up taking her bedroom candle with her, but noticing that it was flickering when she followed the figure into the drawing room she picked up a pink candle there to replace her own.

In the drawing room the figure turned and spoke a single word to Mrs Goodeve – 'Tomorrow' – and vanished and Mrs Goodeve went back to bed. Afterwards Mrs Goodeve said that the figure had passed through the locked drawing room door but she had no recollection of how she herself had followed into the room. Next day the maid was positive that the drawing room door had been locked as usual, but a partly burned pink candle from the drawing room was found in Mrs Goodeve's bedroom candlestick.

When Mrs Goodeve told Mr Ackland what had happened he suggested she should speak to Dr Marshall, a trustee of the house, and when she described the apparition the doctor thought it sounded very much like Mrs Seagrim who had died there some years before, especially since after her death the house was reputed to be haunted, and Mrs Seagrim's daughter had once seen the ghost of her mother.

Mrs Goodeve bravely refused to change her room as she thought it would be cowardly, but agreed to have a bell put under her pillow. That night she was determined to wait up to see if the apparition returned, but eventually fell asleep.

She woke to find the same figure standing by her bed, looking agitated. She said, 'I have come, listen,' and then asked Mrs Goodeve to do something which Mrs Goodeve later refused to divulge. In spite of her apparent calmness, she must have felt increasingly bewildered by what was happening, so that she exclaimed, 'Am I dreaming, or is this true?' And the figure she now believed to be Mrs Seagrim then said, 'If you doubt me, you will find that the date of my marriage was 26th September 1860.'

Mrs Goodeve then became aware that a tall, dark man, about 60 years old, was standing by Mrs Seagrim. He told Mrs Goodeve that he was Henry Barnard and he was buried in Snettisham churchyard, and like Mrs Seagrim, by way of proof he gave Mrs Goodeve the dates of his marriage and death, which she afterwards wrote down in her pocket book.

Henry Barnard asked Mrs Goodeve to go to Snettisham and verify these dates in the church registers, and if she found them correct, she was to go to the church the following morning at 1.15 am and wait beside the grave of a certain Robert Cobb who had died on 15th May 1743, aged 67.

This astonishing conversation continued with the ghost of Henry Barnard telling Mrs Goodeve that when she travelled down to Snettisham by train, the outgoing half of her ticket would not be taken from her at the station and, when there, she would be helped by a dark man and given lodgings in the house of a woman whose child had been drowned and who was buried in the same churchyard as himself.

It is difficult to imagine Mrs Goodeve's state of mind at this stage, especially as she then noticed a third phantom, a man obviously in great misery. All three ghosts then disappeared and, feeling faint, Mrs Goodeve just managed to ring the bell, and was found by Mr Ackland, collapsed on the floor.

However, by next morning Mrs Goodeve was determined to pursue this extraordinary matter further, so she first ascertained from the Post Office that there was a village called Snettisham in Norfolk, which she had never heard of before. And through Dr Marshall, who knew Mrs Seagrim's daughter, the date of Mrs Seagrim's marriage in India was checked, and the date given by the ghost was found to be correct.

So Mrs Goodeve returned home to London, and next morning set off for Snettisham. As the ghost had foretold, there was no one at the station to take her ticket, and Mrs Goodeve sent it to Dr Marshall afterwards as proof of the spirit's accuracy. He, just in case Mrs Goodeve had bought two tickets herself, made enquiries and found that hers had been the only first class ticket to Snettisham from

London that day, and the ticket collector could not account for why it had not been collected.

Owing to a fair there, hotels were full, and Mrs Goodeve found lodgings at the house of the parish clerk, John Bishop, who she realised was the dark man the ghost had described, and his wife later told her that a child of theirs had been drowned, and was buried in the churchyard.

Everything was happening as the ghost of Henry Barnard had described and the next day being Sunday Mrs Goodeve attended the church service and afterwards was able to see the registers and check the dates of Henry Barnard's marriage and death, which were as he had said. She had confided in John Bishop and described the ghost which he at once recognised as Henry Barnard, the late owner of Cobb Hall, whom he had known. He took her to see Barnard's grave and also showed her the tombstone covering the grave of Robert Cobb in the church.

So far Mrs Goodeve's strange adventure had gone exactly as her ghostly visitors had foretold, but now, however embarrassing it might be, she had to obtain permission from the curate to enter the church in the early hours of next morning to keep her assignation with the ghost of one of the former parishioners of Snettisham. As the Rev Maitland said, such a request had probably never been made before of any clergyman; it sounded so preposterous and not surprisingly the curate refused. However, although frail and elderly, Mrs Goodeve was richly dressed and obviously respectable, not to mention determined, and the curate unbent sufficiently to remark to John Bishop that he, of course, also possessed a key and could do as he liked.

That night at about 1 am when Mrs Goodeve and

John Bishop set off for the church she was secretly wondering if she could go through with her daunting rendezvous. But she resolved that she was not prepared to fail at this stage, and after Bishop had searched the church to make sure no one was there, he put out the light and locked her in at about 1.20 am, as she wished.

According to her own testimony, she waited by the grave of Robert Cobb as arranged, and saw the man she had come to see and received the promised message. John Bishop opened the church door for her at about 1.45, after which she went back to bed and slept soundly!

Mrs Goodeve kept the message to herself, but did say that she had been instructed to pluck some white roses from the bushes growing round Barnard's grave and give them to his daughter at Cobb Hall, with the message from her father. This she did the next morning, and had a long interview with Miss Barnard, after which she told Mr Bishop her task was done and she went home, after paying him handsomely for his help.

This story leaves the reader full of questions. No wonder that Andrew Lang, writer and ghost-hunter, confessed himself baffled by the whole affair.

Many ghost stories involve a restless spirit, still troubled after death by conscience or some unfinished business in the world they have left behind. The Rev Maitland says that before Henry Barnard acquired Cobb Hall, it had been in Chancery for many years, and according to local rumour some sort of title had to be patched up before he was able to buy it. So was a dubious property deal so troubling Henry Barnard, and also the sad ghost of Robert Cobb, that they had approached Mrs Goodeve, a lady of psychic sensitivity and indomitable courage, to act on their behalf in an attempt to right some wrong?

And where did the ghost of Mrs Seagrim fit in? Apparently she was a member of the Cobb family, and so could be assumed to be interested and the Rev Maitland suggests that it was not until the arrival of Mrs Goodeve at Mrs Seagrim's former home that her ghost was able to make contact with someone able and willing to help.

When I visited the churchyard at Snettisham I identified the Barnard family burial plot through a photograph in the Rev Maitland's booklet. It is a large, square area surrounded by a low iron fence but, alas, no rose bushes grow there now. I also found the stone marking Robert Cobb's grave in the church with its coat of arms, and imagined Mrs Goodeve's emotions that October night in 1893 when she stood on the same spot in the dark waiting for the ghost of a man she had never known in life.

Just before writing his booklet the Rev Maitland had contacted the only person concerned with the story still alive. This was John Bishop's son who had been a young boy at the time Mrs Goodeve came to Snettisham, but after her return home to London he had been to stay with her several times.

He said that whatever the secret was, his mother was the only person in whom Mrs Goodeve had confided. 'She died twenty years ago', he wrote, 'without having divulged anything, not even to my father.'

It is unlikely that we may ever discover the secret that Henry Barnard was so anxious to pass on to his daughter, or whether his mind was subsequently put at rest. The roses on his grave are long gone, but this strange story of Snettisham a hundred or so years ago is unforgettable.

8

Timeslips

Timeslip One

IF POWERFUL and often tragic events can leave some kind of paranormal record imprinted on the place where they once took place, perhaps it is not surprising that several famous old battlefields have a strange reputation.

After the battle of Edgehill in 1642, one of the bloodiest battles of the Civil War, a ghostly re-enactment was witnessed on several occasions, full of the sights and sounds of conflict, and some of King Charles's officers were able to recognise some of their own friends who had taken part.

The battle of Naseby a few years later, when Cromwell triumphed over the Royalists, produced an amazing spectacle in the sky on the anniversary of the battle, watched regularly by local people for many years.

And phantom soldiers and horsemen from the Duke of Monmouth's defeated army have been seen in flight from the battle of Sedgemoor, which took place in 1685. Many people have testified that on the night of 6th July, the anniversary of Monmouth's defeat, they have seen Monmouth himself riding hell for leather away from the battlefield.

How can these strange spectacles from the past be

explained? Is the witness like a ghost from the future, somehow able to see the past as it really happened, or is it some phantom action replay? And, if so, what triggers such a happening? One night Mr and Mrs Reeves were returning home at about 2.30 am after visiting friends. There was a full moon, but it was becoming rather misty as they drove down the hill to their home in the village of Holme Hale.

Mrs Reeves got out of the car, and as she opened the door she thought she could hear someone shouting for help. Her husband couldn't hear anything but then from the direction of the bridge a few hundred yards down the road, they could both hear shouting, the sound of people running and the noise of galloping horses. It seemed likely that the horses had got out from a nearby farm, and Mr Reeves was preparing to do what he could to help intercept them.

The commotion was getting nearer, but standing there in the road Mr and Mr Reeves could see nothing to account for it. Before long the sounds were all round them, sounding like sticks hitting swords, accompanied by more shouting, and the Reeves cringed back to get out of the way of this invisible battle, with the alarming impression that horses were rearing up almost on top of them.

'It was amazing', Mrs Reeves reported later, 'and so vivid. I can feel it all again as I talk about it.'

Eventually the noise of battle moved away over the hill, fading away into the distance, leaving the husband and wife shocked and puzzled by their experience.

When BBC television investigated the Reeves' experience for their *Timeslip* series, they could not discover any record of a pitched battle at Holme Hale, but the most likely connection was a conflict at the time of Kett's Rebellion in 1549, when some of the rebels retreating from Castle Rising to Watton would have passed through Holme Hale. They were attacked by troops under the command of Sir Edmund Knyvett at their camp in Hingham not far away, the peasants fighting off the soldiers' swords with their wooden staves.

Reading about the incident reminded me of something which happened to me which I described in my book *Ghosts of Hertfordshire.*

I live very close to Bernards Heath, St Albans, and one day as I walked towards the more wooded part of the Common with my dog, I noticed something odd about the trees. They were completely still, with no movement in the leaves or branches, resembling a painted theatrical backdrop, and everywhere seemed unnaturally quiet.

I walked on into the trees and suddenly, without warning, all hell broke loose. I could feel movement all round me, with shouting and the clash of metal so close that I threw my arms up above my head to protect myself. I could hear neighing, and felt as if horses were rearing up almost on top of me, but there was absolutely nothing to see which made it more terrifying.

As I whirled round to get away, there in front of me with his back to a tree sat a man. He was wearing a leather cap and jerkin, boots and some sort of leggings, and he had a bow and arrows. He was holding his head in his hands, and I could tell that he was wounded and in pain. I felt that he was completely unaware of me, and as I looked at him he began to fade, and I realised I could see the trunk of the tree through him, and seconds later he had vanished.

I found myself out of the trees with the feel of the breeze on my face and the sound of birds and the traffic on the nearby road just as usual. My dog came running towards me and as we walked home I tried to come to terms with what had happened and find some rational explanation. I knew that an important battle of the Wars of the Roses took place on Bernards Heath in 1461 when Warwick's Yorkist troops were defeated by the Lancastrian forces who heavily outnumbered them. Did I somehow walk into a re-enactment of part of that battle which happened on the Common more than 500 years ago? Nothing like that has ever happened to me again on the Common, nor, I believe, to anyone else, but I am convinced that it did happen, leaving questions that are impossible to answer.

Timeslip Two . . . Or Was It?

There are many stories of phantom buildings seen briefly before they vanish, or sometimes appearing to be quite a normal part of the surroundings, but next time the witness passes that way they have mysteriously disappeared. And, quite often, enquiries prove that nothing of the kind ever was there!

In her book *The Mask of Time*, Joan Forman mentions a Mr Squirrel who had a curious experience in Great Yarmouth one day in 1973.

Mr Squirrel was a coin collector, and he went into Great Yarmouth to buy some of those small transparent envelopes for keeping individual coins. He had been recommended to a shop where he could get some, and when he went in, he did notice that although the shop was smartly painted outside, inside it seemed rather old-fashioned, particularly the till.

A young woman came forward to serve him. She was wearing a long skirt and blouse with a cameo brooch at the neck, and her hair was drawn back in a bun, but to Mr Squirrel her appearance did not seem particularly dated. She produced the kind of envelopes he wanted, commenting that they were often used by fishermen to keep their hooks in. He bought 36 envelopes and went home.

Finding that he needed some more envelopes, he went back to the shop the next week, but was puzzled to find that the cobbles he remembered outside the shop had now been replaced by paving slabs, and the shop's appearance now seemed drab and dingy. A much older woman came forward to serve him, and was unable to supply him with the envelopes he wanted. She said they didn't stock them and, in fact, never had, and when he mentioned the assistant he had seen the previous week, she said they had never had a young lady like that working there, in fact she had been the only assistant there for many years. It was all very curious.

However, Mr Squirrel had the envelopes he bought on his first visit to the shop, and these were shown to the manufacturers. According to Mr Squirrel's recollections, the shop seemed to date from the early 1900s and the envelopes were certainly not of this period.

The manufacturers believed they were ten or fifteen years old, although cellulose film was used in the 1920s. It was all very curious and Joan Forman suggested that the envelopes seemed to eliminate the possibility that Mr Squirrel had experienced a timeslip. His grandfather had also been a coin collector, and possibly might have visited the same shop. Had his grandson somehow tuned in to a sort of 'family memory'? Or had Mr Squirrel actually visited two different shops?

He did mention noticing a strange quietness when he was in the first shop. There were none of the usual traffic noises from the street outside, and this is a phenomenon often noticed during paranormal experiences. It would be interesting to know if he made any further efforts to see if he had made a mistake in the location. Was it a case of another time or another place? Or did Mr Squirrel actually go shopping in a time before he was born?

9

The Busiest Ghost in England

THERE CAN be few spectres with more claim to this title than Anne Boleyn whose list of personal appearances includes almost everywhere she lived in her short life. Several places such as Bollin Hall in Cheshire, Hever Castle in Kent and Blickling Hall in Norfolk claim to have been her birthplace, all with stories of sightings of Anne's ghost, and not surprisingly the Tower of London where she met her death on 19th May 1536 claims the most dramatic Boleyn hauntings.

Handsome Jacobean Blickling Hall, now owned by the National Trust, is built on the site of a moated manor house where Anne's father Thomas Boleyn lived, and it is likely that Anne spent part of her childhood there. Every year on the anniversary of her death Anne is said to travel up the long avenue to Blickling in a carriage driven by a headless coachman, sitting inside and nursing her head on her lap. On arrival she enters the Hall to wander its rooms and corridors, sometimes as a shadowy 'grey lady', sometimes unseen with only the rustle of her skirts to testify to her presence.

Her father Thomas also frequents the Blickling neighbourhood where, cursed to haunt for a thousand years, his spectral coach must drive over twelve bridges between Blickling and Wroxham Broad on the night of the date of his daughter's execution. Not surprisingly, local people give this area a miss at this time, as Thomas, with his head under his arm, gushing flames from its mouth, is pursued by a fearsome pack of screaming fiends.

Blickling Hall is, of course, the perfect place for a Halloween Tour and in 1998 a former Administrator, Denis Mead, regaled the local newspaper with the various other-worldly sights and sounds he describes to hopeful ghost-hunters. It is all treated in a lighthearted spirit but, given the setting, no doubt more than one nervous visitor takes a quick look over their shoulder, just in case.

Gregorian chants have been heard in the Brown Room, an old Jacobean family chapel, and sepulchral groans in the west turret are attributed to the 4th Earl who died there after fighting a duel on nearby Cawston Heath 300 years ago. The delightful scent of wild violets puzzled a cub scout akela just twenty or so years ago when she was taking part in a 'sleep in' at the mausoleum. Could the fact that the 2nd Earl's wife used to pick these flowers to make perfume centuries earlier have had anything to do with it?

And inevitably there is a ghostly black dog which haunts the woodland. Although spectral black dogs are part of Norfolk history, this is not Black Shuck but a 17th century gamekeeper's dog found sitting by his dead master who had bled to death after an accident. At the time staff wrongly assumed that the dog had savaged the keeper, and he was destroyed, but his wraith still roams the woods he used to know.

But, of course, the ghost everyone wants to hear about

is Blickling's grey lady, poor ill-fated Anne Boleyn. She still sometimes puts in an appearance, such as the time a member of staff was walking down the Long Gallery library when she noticed a grey figure sitting there, looking at a book. As she drew nearer, the figure faded away, leaving the book lying open on the table, and she found that it was a collection of Holbein portraits – open at the picture of Anne Boleyn!

Denis Mead cheerfully admits that he has never seen a ghost despite his many years in one of Britain's most haunted stately homes. But he came within minutes of a close encounter with Blickling's most famous wraith one night. I met a long time colleague of his when I visited Blickling in 1999 who told me all about this remarkable happening.

It appears that a portrait of Queen Elizabeth I had been sent away for restoration in the 1960s, but when it was being returned, the vehicle bringing it back had broken down, so that it was almost midnight before it arrived at Blickling and the driver carried the portrait into the dining room.

Mr Mead, who ran the Hall from 1961 to 1982, arrived with an assistant and asked the delivery man if he wanted a signature for the picture. But the man replied, 'No, that's all right, the lady in the grey dress has already done it.'

'We thought he was pulling our legs', said Mr Mead, 'as we knew there was no one else here.'

Even so they checked the house and all the alarms and everything was in order, and there was no one to be seen. And then they realised it was now past midnight and the anniversary of Anne Boleyn's execution! By then the delivery man had gone, but not surprisingly next morning the firm that had restored the picture rang to say they had no signature for the delivery!

Some strange happenings defy explanation. After more than 450 years, is the ghost of Henry VIII's tragic Queen really still pursuing her round of hauntings year after year? It would be nice to think that, bored with her usual drive with the headless coachman, she is capable of a mischievous trick or two!

When I visited Blickling I was told that she had sometimes been seen down by the lake. Apparently one day the then National Trust Administrator, Mr Sidney Hancock, noticed a woman walking by the lakeside, and thinking she was either lost or trespassing he went to speak to her. She was wearing a long grey gown with a white lace collar and a white cap, and he asked her if he could help, or was she looking for someone? Her answer was: 'That for which I seek has long since gone.'

Mr Hancock momentarily looked away, but when he turned back he found there was no one there!

So if you should visit Blickling, keep an eye open. That lady in grey in the library or strolling by the lake may not be quite what she seems.

10

The Lady in the Chair

If places where tragedy, drama and powerful emotion have occurred are sometimes the setting for a psychic replay of those events, what of inanimate objects? Could a chair for instance retain a haunting memory of the past?

The chair in the following strange story came to the attention of a lady who was sheltering in the doorway of an old curiosity shop in Nottingham in a thunderstorm shortly after the First World War.

Suddenly she heard a voice crying 'Save me! Save me!' which seemed to come from inside the shop. She turned to look into the window, and although the interior of the shop was rather dark, she could see a woman with red hair and a richly handsome gown sitting in a chair. Opening the shop door, she heard the woman cry out 'Save me!' yet again, but at that moment the proprietor of the shop appeared, and as she looked towards the chair she saw that it was now empty.

The lady was Mrs Mary Hutt, wife of Canon Hutt, sometime Rector of Bingham in Nottinghamshire, and to cover her confusion at this extraordinary happening, she asked the price of the chair. It was just a few shillings so she purchased it, the proprietor volunteering the information that it had come from Newstead Abbey.

Mrs Hutt had arranged to meet her chauffeur who collected the chair and they set off for home but the journey was not without incident. Without warning the car repeatedly veered across the road as if the steering was faulty, which apparently was not the case. And next day Mrs Hutt asked her maid to give the rather dirty chair a good wash, but the girl came to her later and said she couldn't do it as she thought the chair was bewitched. Apparently Mrs Hutt then scrubbed the chair herself, but thereafter whenever it was placed near a firegrate, whether or not the fire was alight, the red-haired ghost appeared sitting in it.

After her husband's death, Mrs Hutt moved to Norfolk, and the day after her move she was busy putting loose covers on her chairs when her little dog rushed to the window, barking excitedly. Thinking someone must be coming, Mrs Hutt looked out of the window and there was the familiar ghostly figure coming up her drive. She realised that the removal men had placed the haunted chair in the fireplace, and at that moment the ghost entered the room and sat in her chair!

When Mrs Hutt died, she left the haunted chair to Bryan Hall of Banningham Rectory who was an old family friend, with the proviso that he should never place it near a fire. I asked Mr Hall if he ever had, and he laughed and said, 'I wouldn't dare risk it, I've kept it well away from the fire.' However, he said that even on a warm summer's day, people standing near the chair have commented on what a very cold spot it is. And when he sent someone with a van to fetch the chair when it first came into his possession, they had the same experience as Mrs Hutt's chauffeur, as the van behaved erratically on the way back as if the steering was faulty.

The chair is a pretty shape and is painted in cream and gold with a flower decoration. It has a cane seat and the back has a delicate Sheraton-style lattice. What is its history, and what was the peril that the red-haired lady so desperately wanted to be saved from? And as the chair came from Newstead Abbey, was she perhaps a member of the Byron family?

Newstead Abbey belonged to the Byron family who acquired it in 1540 after the Dissolution of the Monasteries and, as he left, the Abbot cursed the Abbey and all who would live there in the future. Misfortune subsequently afflicted the family, and by the time the famous poet inherited Newstead in 1798 their fortunes were at a low ebb and the building was in a rundown condition, mainly due to the wild and wicked activities of William, the 5th Lord Byron. The Abbey was haunted by what is called the Black or Goblin Friar, a spectre seen by Byron on the eve of his marriage to Anne Milbanke in 1815, which convinced him that their union would not be a happy one, since tradition had it that the ghost appeared to the head of the Byron family before any misfortune.

Certainly tragedy, debt and scandal in the Byron family seem to have fulfilled the old Abbot's curse, but whatever it was that distressed the red-haired lady in the chair we may never know.

Bryan Hall is no stranger to the supernatural. His home dates back to the 17th century, and he told me that when a psychic group visited some time ago they left recording machines in some of the rooms. One had recorded a curious rocking sound and a human sigh – 'I realised the noise was the sound of a cradle rocking,' he said. In another room the machine had recorded a sound like crunching on gravel which the investigators could not identify, but Mr Hall recognised the sound of horse's hooves. 'People say that round here was Cromwell's land', he told me, 'and I'm sure the Parliamentarians came to this house.'

Mr Hall used to sleep in the largest bedroom in the house in a fourposter, and he told me about one strange experience he had. One day a friend of his who deals in antiquarian books brought a curious object for him to see. 'It appeared to be bone like a section of an animal's vertebrae and it was painted with a representation of the Devil. From its appearance it looked as if it had been well handled over many years, and I felt instinctively that there was something evil about it. He was asking £2 for it, and I can't think why I did, but I bought it from him,' he said.

'I felt uneasy as I took it up to my room. Then in the early hours of the next morning I woke up suddenly. I was drowsy and half asleep when suddenly without warning it was as if two pairs of arms had gone underneath my mattress and before I could do anything to help myself the mattress was lifted up and I was thrown out onto the floor. I felt sure that the thing I had bought from my friend had something to do with it, and I couldn't wait to throw it away. I felt shaken for quite a long time afterwards.'

In my book *Ghosts of Suffolk* I wrote about a haunted portrait of Henrietta Nelson which was unfortunately stolen from Bryan Hall's home in an armed robbery in 1995. Mr Hall had owned the picture for nearly 50 years, but had known the strange story of Henrietta and her portrait since his youth. Miss Nelson died at Yaxley Hall in

Suffolk in 1816 at the age of 82 after falling downstairs. According to tradition, she had a strong objection to being buried in the family vault, and a mausoleum was built for her in the Hall grounds.

There Henrietta rested peacefully until a new owner decided to demolish the mausoleum and remove her to the family vault, and after this her restless spirit was seen wandering in the garden and grounds. When the picture passed to different owners it became apparent that wherever Henrietta's portrait went her ghost would follow, and she was seen dressed as in her portrait but her face and clothing were the colour of parchment. Mr Hall had owned the portrait since the early 1950s when he bought it at an auction, and subsequently there were reported sightings of Henrietta's ghost walking in the grounds of his home.

It was also noticed that her portrait had a startling ability to change expression. 'As a portrait it was fascinating, the face was very much alive,' Mr Hall said. He continued sadly that after the robbery the house seemed curiously empty, and he felt sure Henrietta's spirit had left with the picture.

11

The Haunting of 19 Magdalen Street

SOME OF the most interesting ghost stories concern premises such as pubs or shops which change hands from time to time, and yet each newcomer soon comes to realise that they are apparently sharing the property with a longtime resident who has no intention of moving on.

A certain building in Magdalen Street, Norwich is still remembered as a place of ill repute when it was a pub, and the story is that a young girl called Sara was murdered there in Victorian times. If this is true it may account for the strange happenings which have repeatedly disturbed occupants of the building which was turned into commercial property some years ago. Who was Sara and why did she meet such an unhappy fate that her restless spirit has remained earthbound?

As a shop No 19 has had many occupants, among them Radio Rentals followed by an Oxfam charity shop, in both of which the staff experienced odd happenings. If the incoming staff of Oxfam were warned that a figure had been seen at the foot of the stairs, and that sometimes the air in the shop became unnaturally cold for no apparent reason, they probably dismissed such stories as of little importance.

And yet, quite soon they too experienced noticeably cold spots in certain areas, and there were sudden icy draughts upstairs where they had their office when there was no open window or door to account for it.

This front upper room seemed to be the focus for the disturbing happenings, one of the most alarming being when a secretary walked in to find her typewriter working of its own accord. She couldn't believe her eyes as she saw the keys moving up and down as if tapped by an invisible hand, and she had the chilling sensation that she was not alone. This feeling of an unseen presence was frequently experienced by members of the staff, and footsteps were heard on the stairs when no one was there.

Naturally these inexplicably eerie happenings aroused local interest and no less than three psychical research societies investigated the building, and they were all convinced that paranormal influences were at work. This was reported in the press, and the newspaper cutting was pinned to the wall of the office. Soon afterwards a member of staff came in to find the cutting swinging rhythmically to and fro on its pin, but there was no breeze from an open window to cause it, and other notices pinned alongside were quite still!

The member of staff reached out and stopped the cutting's gyrations for a moment, but as soon as he released it, the swinging started up again. Sensibly the cutting was then secured more firmly with drawing pins top and bottom and that did the trick!

In her book *Haunted East Anglia*, Joan Forman describes her visit to the shop during Oxfam's occupation, and the strong sensation of a presence that she felt in the upstairs office, a feeling she found oppressive and uncomfortable.

At the time that I was researching this book, 19

Magdalen Street was occupied by Ron's Reptiles, and when I talked to the proprietor he told me of a recent experience of his own there. He was there by himself late one night and at about 3 am he was sitting in the kitchen in a recess just behind the fire exit when suddenly without warning, the 'Fire Exit' sign dropped down and hit him a glancing blow on the side of his head.

The strange thing was that where he was sitting the sign was above, and to the right of him, and yet it hit him on the left side of his head!

'It was as if it swung in front of me as it dropped', he said, 'just as if it had been deliberately moved not just accidentally dropped.'

His wife has sometimes noticed noises overhead when no one was up there, and is conscious at times of an unseen presence. Like other occupants before, she has encountered definite cold spots, and when this happens there is an overwhelming smell of lavender.

Dave Chisnell who organises the Norwich Ghost Walk has also had experience of Magdalen Street's fragrant phantom when he and his group have stopped outside No 19. 'I have lost count of the number of people who have told met they smell lavender outside the building,' says Dave. 'One lady came up afterwards and said "I loved all the stunts, but the best was the lavender smell. How do you do that?" Even my father asked if we dropped lavender pellets, but we don't at all.'

Perhaps Sara gets lonely when the shop is closed for the night, and wanders outside in search of company. Undoubtedly the lavender scent seems to be the pleasantest trick in the repertoire of the sad little ghost of No 19 Magdalen Street, Norwich.

12

The White Ladies of Norfolk

WOLTERTON HALL is an elegant house which has suffered various unfortunate periods such as military occupation during the last war, a disastrous fire in 1952, the discovery of dry rot, and times when it was left unoccupied and neglected and many of its valuable contents sold.

At present restoration work is taking place, and part of the building is used for estate offices, but some of the rooms are open to visitors at certain times and I was lucky to be in the area one day when the house was open for a conducted tour.

My chief interest was, of course, the family ghost, Wolterton's White Lady, said to appear whenever some calamity threatens the family. According to Lady Dorothy Nevill, author of *Mannington and the Walpoles* published in 1894, a large Conversation Piece was painted showing Ambassador Horace Walpole and his wife Mary (Lombard) and several children. However, Lady Dorothy's father Horatio Walpole, the 3rd Earl, cut up the picture and gave the pieces to different members of the family who were descendants of those portrayed! And according to Lady Dorothy it is this act of vandalism that causes the ghost of

Mary Walpole to haunt Wolterton 'seeking for her divided relatives'.

However, Lady Dorothy also says that her brother, Lord Orford, said to her one day, 'I hear from Norfolk that the White Lady has been seen again. It is you or I this time Dolly, for we are the only ones left.' He died shortly afterwards in 1894.

When I visited Wolterton Hall I asked Lady Walpole about the White Lady and she said that her husband's grandmother remembered that one night there was a knocking on the front door, but when it was opened there was no one outside. Shortly afterwards they heard that the Earl of Orford had died in New Zealand. This was in the 1930s.

At Old Catton, near Norwich, there is a narrow road known as White Woman Lane where a figure in white has often been seen crossing and re-crossing just as dusk is falling. The ghost is believed to be a daughter of the local Manor House who fell in love with one of her father's coachmen whose home was on the opposite side of the lane from the Manor. The story goes that she used to steal out secretly at night to visit him, which suggests the usual tragedy of forbidden love between a lady of the Manor and a sweetheart considered by her family to be far beneath her. Their story must have had a sad ending, or she would no longer haunt the lane where once she hurried to her secret rendezvous.

Yet another distraught White Lady haunts an area at Aylmerton where a number of hollows in the ground are believed to be ancient iron-working pits. These are known as the Shrieking Pits as the sad phantom of a woman in white has been seen passing from one pit to another, weeping as she peers into each and shrieking with anguish when she fails to find what she is seeking.

It is said that she is looking for her baby, buried in one of the pits by her husband who murdered them both in a fit of mad jealousy in the 19th century.

The ancient church of St Mary at Worstead has a long standing ghost story concerning a White Lady said to make her appearance on Christmas Eve when the bells are rung at midnight to celebrate the birth of Our Lord.

There is, of course, always someone foolhardy enough to scoff at such stories, and apparently in 1830 a local man declared himself willing to climb into the belfry in search of the ghost, and if he met her he said he would give her a kiss.

So off he went, his friends waiting nervously below as he climbed up into the tower. It seemed very quiet and after a while they called up to him, but there was no answering shout and they decided to go up to see what had happened.

He was there in the belfry, lying huddled in a heap and apparently lifeless. They carried him down and took him to the nearby inn where he recovered sufficiently to whisper 'I've seen her! I've seen her!' and then expired.

We can never know just what happened that night in the old belfry. But in her *Norfolk Ghosts & Legends*, Polly Howat tells the story of something strange which happened in the 1970s. Someone who lived locally was in the church and happened to notice a woman, apparently in some distress, praying by the font, and he saw her husband take a photograph of her.

Several months later a copy of the print was sent to someone connected with the church, and it was seen by the same local man who recognised the woman he had observed praying. The strange feature of the photograph was the fact that close behind her could be seen the clear impression of a woman wearing a bonnet and ankle length smock. As the local man knew, no one of this kind had been standing behind the woman in prayer when the picture was taken, and yet it looked quite real. Had the photograph been tampered with as a hoax?

Two years later, when he was again in the church, the same visitor arrived and spoke to him. She said that she had visited the church two years previously when she was ill and troubled and had prayed for help, and God had answered her through the presence of a woman who had stood over her. She produced a copy of the photograph he had seen before, showing the presence of another woman standing behind her as she prayed.

So did the woman's husband capture a ghost on his photograph? And could it have been the legendary White Lady?

Hickling Broad, as you can read in Chapter 5, has a famous ghost, the skating soldier. But it appears that he is not the only manifestation on this stretch of water.

A couple were in their cruiser on Hickling Broad one night. As they knew, they should not have been moving in the dark, but they were anxious to get to their berth. They were very concerned when they noticed a woman punting towards them. The man shouted to warn her but she appeared to ignore him and they were horrified as it seemed that they could not avoid running into her.

They were both relieved and astonished to then see that the punt had now reappeared on the other side of their boat, just as if it had passed straight through them, and the woman in white was still apparently quite oblivious of them as she disappeared in the darkness.

They berthed and went into a nearby pub and in the course of conversation told the landlord what had happened. He showed no surprise. The lady in the punt was apparently a local ghost who regularly punted across from a mill on one side of the water to the other. Just who she was and where she was going are apparently unknown. She is just one more of Norfolk's mysterious White Ladies.

13

Haunted Hostelries

Every Twenty Years

THE OLD Ferry Inn at Horning by the river Bure is a well-known pub where the water is full of craft in the summertime. But if you hope to see the legendary ghost of Horning, you only have a slim chance of being at the right place at the right time.

The original 15th century building, which received a direct hit from a German bomb in 1941, was a mead storehouse for nearby St Bene't's Abbey and one day a number of monks had sampled rather too much of the brew when a pretty local girl happened to walk by. Their vows forgotten, they seized and raped her, and in a frenzy of fear that their crime would be discovered, they murdered her and threw her body into the river.

Once every twenty years, on 25th September, she is said to appear. One recorded sighting was in 1936 when the licensee was in the inn at about midnight, awaiting the return of a resident. He was dozing when something woke him. 'I heard a noise, a rustling,' he said. 'Not three yards from me, in the passage leading to the staircase, was the frail shadowy form of a girl about 25. She wore a greenish grey cloak but it was her face that attracted my attention. It was beautiful yet deathly white, and had a look of suffering. I spoke to her and went towards her, but she glided in front of me towards the door. She appeared to go through the door. I opened it and followed, and was just in time to see her disappear at the edge of the river near the chain ferry.'

Another resident happened to be outside and was able to corroborate the landlord's story. He heard him cry out, and the next moment he saw the slim figure of a girl glide past him and into the water.

The Tudor Rose Hotel, King's Lynn

This is situated in a very old part of the area which dates back to the 12th century and in the past, when the building was almost derelict, it was locally known as the 'Haunted House' or 'Haunted Castle' and not the kind of place anyone liked to pass late at night.

The story goes that a horrific murder took place during a wedding party. After the ceremony the guests were celebrating in the building, but having drunk too many toasts, a quarrel arose in the course of which the bridegroom stabbed his bride to death. Another version of the story has the bride's jilted lover bursting into the celebrations and killing both bride and groom in a fit of mad jealousy. A presence, thought to be the murdered bride, is said to haunt the hotel still. Mrs Sally Hunter, who lived at the Tudor Rose from 1977 to 1984, took little notice of stories that the place was haunted, until one busy winter evening when she asked a waitress to go down from the restaurant to the bar to fetch a glass of port for a customer.

The waitress seemed to be taking rather a long time, so she went to the top of the stairs to call her. She was somewhat shocked to see not the waitress, but a small woman in a long pale dress coming up the stairs towards her. Her face was infinitely sad, and although she looked quite solid, there was something ethereal about her, and as Mrs Hunter looked at her, she disintegrated into mist.

At that point the waitress appeared with the port, flapping her hands vigorously as she remarked 'It isn't half smoky on the stairs', and walked right through the still visible mist. Mrs Hunter noticed that a depressing atmosphere seemed to linger for about two days.

A number of other things happened such as glasses being taken from the shelves and put on the floor, and a heavy tray was found smashed. Once during a snowfall a receptionist reported that someone was clearing the snow away in the yard, but when Mrs Hunter went to thank him, there was no one there and the snow was untouched. One woman often noticed footsteps behind her but when she looked there was no one there, and once when Mrs Hunter's two-year-old daughter had gone upstairs, her mother followed and found that the light on the stairs had been switched on. The switch was too high for the child to reach, but when Mrs Hunter asked who had switched it on, the little girl replied, 'The lady did.'

The young son of subsequent proprietors said he had seen the ghost of a nun in his bedroom in 1996. There is a tradition that centuries ago there was a nunnery there, but a veiled figure could equally perhaps be the shade of the murdered bride.

The Duke's Head Hotel, Yarmouth

Dating back many centuries, this inn has long been reputed to be haunted. The cellar seems to be a focal point for much of the paranormal activity where the gas bottles used to pump beer up to the bar turn themselves on and off without human aid. The lighting in the cellar also turns on and off and a video recorder is often busy recording programmes of its own accord, although which are the unseen presence's favourites is not known. The X Files perhaps?

The usual mischievous tricks have been played on a succession of landlords as watches, cigarette lighters, pens and keys have disappeared and reappeared somewhere unexpected, and the torch one landlord kept by his bedside went missing and was ultimately found in a locked box at the bottom of the wardrobe!

The Duke's Head is a popular venue for ghost-hunters to stage sponsored sit-ins but who is the spirit of the cellar who seems to terrify the bravest dog? Well, an old book called *Tales and Traditions of Old Yarmouth*, dated 1893, may offer a clue.

According to legend, a certain Baron Rudolph Scarfe, a wicked and depraved German, was notorious in the 13th century for his evil deeds and was eventually forced to seek asylum in England. Eventually he settled near Burgh Castle and began to terrorise the people of Yarmouth. The book says that Catholic priests imprisoned him in the vaults of the Duke's Head 'for so long a time as the waters flow beneath Yarmouth Bridge'. The old wooden bridge referred to has long since been replaced so is Scarfe still lurking in the Duke's Head cellar?

Another Scarfe legend has him killed by a brave knight, but when he arrived in Hell he was too wicked even for the Devil to admit him, and he was changed into a ferocious black hell-hound with clanking chains and eyes gleaming red like fire.

Understandably he is sometimes confused with Black Shuck, the legendary Hound of Odin which haunts coastal paths and lonely places throughout East Anglia (see Chapter 19). He, too, is big as a calf, black and shaggy, with eyes like glowing coals and to meet him is said to presage death within the year. However Black Shuck, under other names, is known in other parts of the country and is said to have arrived here with the Vikings.

Norwich's Haunted Pubs

The Tap and Spile in Oak Street has experienced the usual poltergeist type happenings. There have been footsteps overhead when no one was up there, and bottles and glasses in the bar have been moved by no human hand.

The pub was formerly known as the White Lion, and one former landlord was one of the last people to be sent to the gallows for the murder of a prostitute. Is he the unseen entity behind those bumps in the night?

Located in Riverside Road, the Bridge House pub is built over a site where underground cells existed in the 16th century. Those dark, damp cellars must have housed many a miserable and troubled soul anxiously awaiting their fate, like many of Wycliffe's followers who were imprisoned there, later to be burned to death in Lollards Pit nearby. It's said that agonised screams can still be heard from time to time.

The Adam and Eve in Bishopsgate is probably the city's oldest pub, dating back to the 13th century when it was built for workmen constructing the cathedral. It is said to be haunted by Lord Sheffield, who met a cruel fate at the time of Kett's Rebellion in 1549. He was sent to crush the peasants' revolt but at the height of the fighting he recklessly removed his helmet and waved it in the air, which gave a local butcher called Fulke the opportunity to strike what proved to be a fatal blow. Lord Sheffield was taken into the inn, where he died. He has, however, continued to make his presence felt; apparently the staff affectionately call him Sam.

The Scole Inn

This 17th century hostelry on the A143 two miles from Diss was once known as the White Hart and was a busy and popular coaching inn in the 17th and 18th centuries. There must have been times when the landlord was hard put to it to accommodate all his guests, but he found an ingenious answer. Room 6 is known as the Sundial Room and a drawing on the wall explains why. The picture may look like a huge sundial but it really depicts a vast circular bed in which up to 30 people could sleep, feet to the centre!

This has nothing to do with the ghost which haunts a room on the first floor, said to be a lady whose jealous husband accused her of being unfaithful to him and murdered her. But who she was seems to have been forgotten over time.

Old Hunstanton's Grey Lady

The Lodge Hotel in Old Hunstanton dates back to smuggling days and there is supposed to be a tunnel leading from the cellars to the beach which the local freeloaders used to transport their booty.

Guests and staff have both been aware of unexplained sounds and an uneasy atmosphere, and some have seen the figure of a little old grey lady moving about the hotel, who disappears rather suddenly through doors and walls! Apparently she doesn't confine herself to the hotel, she has also been seen on an old bridge down the road.

A member of staff reported an alarming experience one evening when she was in a small attic room. She sensed that she was not alone, and heard a rustling sound beside her, and the door which she had wedged open suddenly slammed shut with a bang! She was off downstairs like a shot, and gave that particular room a wide berth after dark in future.

Nearby Hunstanton Hall is also haunted by an old lady – Armine Styleman (see Chapter 3). Could Armine and the ghost of the Lodge Hotel be one and the same?

A Cold Spot in Thorpe Market

It's said that Edward VII kept romantic assignations with the beautiful Lily Langtry in what is now the Elderton Lodge Hotel, in fact her initials are scratched into one of the windowpanes. The building was at that time a hunting lodge, part of the Gunton Hall estate of the Earl of Suffield.

One of the maids there, we are told, once received a severe telling-off from the housekeeper, and the poor girl was so distressed that she hanged herself from the servants' staircase. People have reported a noticeable cold spot at a particular point on this staircase, and some experience a sensation of falling backwards there. There have been sightings of the poor girl standing at the foot of the bed in bedrooms in that area, and some guests say they have felt the bedclothes being tugged in the night.

A Briston 'Regular'

While researching this book I had lunch at the John H. Strachey pub in Briston and discovered that this was yet another Norfolk pub with an unusual 'regular'. The landlord told me he had never seen him himself, but the lounge door opens by itself many times, and they hear footsteps along the landing upstairs when they know no one is up there.

This is an old coaching inn dating back to 1565, and has an L-shaped bar. The landlord said that a few months before one of the girls working in the bar pointed out that there was an old gentleman in the part round the corner waiting to be served. But when the landlord went to attend to him there was no one there. Other customers confirmed that they had seen a grey-haired elderly man with a little beard but he had apparently disappeared! One minute he was there, and the next he had gone, although nobody saw him leave. The pub has, of course, had many alterations over the years, and just by the part of the bar where the elusive customer had been seen there used to be a door which is now blocked off. Obviously it is still useful as an exit for the ghost!

14

Ghosts that Haunt the Royals

IT IS hardly surprising that royalty feature largely among the haunters and the haunted and the palaces of our own Royal Family all have their own stories of the paranormal. From the earliest times, drama and tragedy seem to have provided that vital impression on surroundings that appears to create a haunting, and royal history has never been short of both.

Of all the royal residences, Sandringham's ghosts are the least alarming. There are no screaming queens as at Hampton Court where poor Catherine Howard still pleads with her heartless husband for her life, or visions such as that of the stately figure of Elizabeth I sometimes seen in the library at Windsor. Christmas is the time that Sandringham experiences the mischievous activities of one of their paranormal visitors. Then Christmas cards are moved or even thrown around, the bedclothes are ripped off newly made beds, and the maids have been frightened by something invisible breathing heavily in their ears.

When the usual ghostly shenanigans of switching lights on and off start and there is the sound of footsteps when no one is there, the maids prefer to carry out their duties in pairs. But in her book *Royal Hauntings*, Joan Forman describes a rather charming episode told her by a member of the Royal Family. It was after a period of extensive renovation when an old part of the building had been replaced by modern kitchens. A woman guest woke up one night to see a light in her bedroom, and she was surprised to see the figure of a small boy. He was carrying a long pole which he lifted up every few yards as he walked and she realised he was either lighting or snuffing out invisible candles, just as he must have done in time gone by.

It was the first time anyone had seen this manifestation but appears to be yet another instance of how renovation or rebuilding often seems to encourage supernatural activity.

The Queen is well aware of the ghostly happenings at Sandringham and likes to hear about anything unusual that occurs. In 1996 one of the male servants, Shaun Croasdale, had been down to the cellar to fetch some bottles of wine, when on the way back he suddenly encountered a figure he recognised as Tony Jarred, a former steward. He knew that although Tony looked his familiar self in his blue apron, he had died the previous November, and the shock made Shaun drop the bottles he was carrying and run screaming from the cellar.

The Queen heard about this and sent for him and asked him to tell her what he had seen. She reassured the man who was still rather shaken by his experience, remarking that she had known Tony for much of her life as he had also worked at Buckingham Palace for thirty-eight years. He was such a dedicated servant, she said, that as Shaun had now taken over his duties, probably Tony had returned to keep a friendly eye on him.

Some years ago Prince Christopher of Greece, the Duke of Edinburgh's uncle, was staying at Sandringham and glancing up from the book he was reading he saw the head and shoulders of a woman reflected in his dressing table mirror. She had soft curly brown hair, a dimple in her chin and was wearing a mask. Later he went on a visit to nearby Houghton Hall, and was astonished to see a portrait of the same woman wearing the same dress and a mask. It was Dorothy Walpole, unhappily married to Charles Townshend in the 18th century and destined to become one of England's most famous ghosts, the Brown Lady of Raynham Hall. Houghton Hall was, of course, her childhood home.

15

On the Road

MOST GHOST-HUNTERS would agree that the likeliest place to encounter your average ghost is a stately home, or ye olde village inn, but one night as they are driving along a quiet country lane suddenly someone or something dashes out right in front of the car before they have a chance to stop. Shaken and afraid of what they will see, they get out and find – nothing! Were they dreaming? But it seemed so real, and mixed with their obvious relief that no one has been hurt is the feeling that something did happen. Something strange.

There are some roads where such experiences are common and ghostly jaywalkers, phantom hitch-hikers, shadowy highwaymen and transport of another age emerge out of nowhere to give the modern motorist or pedestrian the fright of their lives . . .

The Great Melton Bridesmaids

Great Melton, six miles from Norwich on the B1108, was once the site of tragedy when four bridesmaids were travelling by night through the village on their way home from a wedding party. As the coach drove along rapidly at great speed it careered off the road, ending up in a deep pond or pit by the roadside, and all the occupants were drowned.

A more dramatic version of the story says that the coach was held up by a highwayman who murdered all the occupants and threw their bodies into the pond. And yet another blames the coachman whose drunken driving caused the coach to lurch off balance and end up in the water.

Whatever the cause of the bridesmaids' unhappy fate, legend has it that from time to time a phantom coach is seen driving at reckless speed along this stretch of road, but beware if you are around when it happens for if the coachman and the bridesmaids are headless, bad luck or worse is in store.

Shipdham

A sadly familiar story from the early 18th century concerns a young maid working at a house in Letton Road who was led astray by the master and sent home in disgrace, but she never arrived. Next day her body was found drowned in a small pond near Blackmoor Road. According to *Haunted Shipdham* by Maurice Woods, the pond often has a misty, eerie look and the maid's ghost can sometimes be seen clutching a bundle of her belongings.

The same booklet tells the story of a farmworker, wrongly accused by a workmate of killing the farmer's prize sheep. He was saved from the gallows by the farmer, but was deported, leaving behind his wife and three children.

His faithful old dog sat at the crossroads where Blackmoor joins Cranworth Road, waiting day after day for his master and refusing to eat, until he died.

Eventually, due to a deathbed confession by the workmate, the man's innocence was proved and he returned home, but unable to find what had happened to his family, he died of a broken heart.

The ghosts of the man and his faithful dog have been seen walking together along the road, and the author of the booklet says that he noticed a man following along behind him late one November afternoon, but when he reached the crossroads and looked round, he had vanished.

Anne Boleyn at Caister Castle

The ruins of Caister Castle, a mile west of Caister-on-Sea, stand alongside a motor museum, but a vintage vehicle of an earlier period is said to arrive at midnight every year on the anniversary of Anne Boleyn's execution. This coach is said to be drawn by four headless horses and driven by a headless coachman, just like the one which conveys Anne Boleyn to Blickling Hall on the same date (see Chapter 9). So what brings the ubiquitous Anne to Caister? The castle belonged to Sir John Fastolf (1378–1459) who once owned Blickling Hall, Anne's childhood home, so perhaps this is why she is said to include the castle in her anniversary tour.

The Christmas Coach at Breckles

On the edge of Breckland in south Norfolk you can see the beautiful old manor house called Breckles Hall. This had a sad history at the time of Dr Augustus Jessop, whose encounter with the Mannington Hall ghost is described in Chapter 17. He said Breckles Hall was 'a house which, for 300 years, no owner seems to have been able to hand down to a grandson of his own . . . it was a house in which two of its owners are said to have committed suicide.'

The Hall's ghost story concerns a sinister coach with its beautiful but evil passenger which arrives there on occasion at midnight, especially at Christmas. If the Hall is empty, the dark windows become suddenly ablaze with light, and anyone brave or foolish enough to look inside will see the gentry of a bygone age in their powdered wigs and finery, dancing merrily to a soundless tune.

The footman jumps from the coach and pulls down the carriage steps for the passenger in her silken gown and jewels to alight. But pity any witness who meets her gaze, for to look into her eyes is sure and certain death.

This story was well known to the locals one Christmas night in the early 1900s when Jim (or George) Mace and some of his cronies announced to the company at the inn that they were off to help themselves to a brace or two of pheasants. The Hall was empty, they knew, so it would be a doddle. But some of their listeners looked dubious, and reminded them of the Christmas coach and the lady whose looks could kill.

This cut no ice with Mace and co, who laughed at such nonsense and went off to poach their Christmas dinner. They arrived in front of the Hall carrying their booty just as the church clock began to strike midnight, and as the last stroke sounded up the drive swept a brightly lit coach and four, and as if at a signal, lights blazed from the Hall's windows. A footman leapt out, pulled down the carriage steps and opened the door for a beautiful lady, dazzling in finery such as the stunned poachers had never seen or imagined.

Mace stood petrified in front of the Hall door and as his

terrified eyes met those of the deadly beauty, he gave just one awful bloodcurdling scream. His friends didn't hesitate, they ran, leaving Mace to his fate, and no one ventured near the Hall until the next day. There had been no sign of Mace, and when a fearful party from the village arrived at the Hall they found the frozen body of Mace lying there in the snow where he had fallen, an agonized expression on his face and his eyes wide and staring.

Apparently the Coroner ordered that poor Jim's eyes should be photographed in case any reflection of the cause of his terrible death remained on the retina, but there was nothing. But no one was in any doubt about the cause of death. Jim Mace had gazed into the eyes of the Lady from Hell and paid the price. They say that news of his bizarre fate travelled far beyond Breckland, and was even reported in *The Times* newspaper!

A Phantom Coach near Ditchingham

In her *Haunted East Anglia*, Joan Forman reports another phantom coach experience which happened to a resident of Brooke village, south of Norwich. The man had been to a meeting in Bungay on the Norfolk-Suffolk border, and was on his way home at about 10.15 pm. He was driving along and had reached a stretch of new concrete road between Ditchingham and Bungay where the old road, now bypassed by the new, veers away at the bottom of the hill and becomes a layby.

The man drove up the hill and was descending on the other side when suddenly to his amazement there was a coach and horses coming full tilt towards him in the middle of the road. He registered that it had four horses and a coachman and possibly a second person beside him, and realised that a head-on collision was almost inevitable. He braked rapidly, but the coach showed no sign of slowing down, and as he desperately tried to avoid it, he said the coach just 'floated away' into the layby and was gone.

It was a hair-raising experience which left the motorist badly shaken. Apparently he mentioned this stretch of road to an old local resident sometime later, and the man remarked that it was known as Lion's Grave, and considered to be a place with an evil reputation. Joan Forman says that 'Grave' is a Norfolk term for a hole in the ground, so was there once a ditch or pond there where a coach once foundered? But why Lion?

16

The Crusaders of Ingham

When I heard about the two Crusaders of Ingham and their deadly rendezvous at Stalham Broad, I couldn't wait to see them. But when I arrived at Holy Trinity church where they lie in stony slumber, I found it padlocked with no information as to the whereabouts of the key. But thanks to Charles Sampson's *Ghosts of the Broads* I have been able to imagine what I was missing.

The church is an ancient one, built upon the site of an even older edifice. According to Charles Sampson, a local inhabitant who recommended a visit told him that 'you goes all goosey all over the very moment you enters the church', and Sampson agreed that the building had a certain chill far beyond the usual cool atmosphere in such a place.

On the north side of the sanctuary stone effigies of Sir Oliver de Ingham and his wife Dame Elizabeth sleep the centuries away on their tomb dated 1343. And at the east end of the nave stands the altar tomb of Sir Roger de Bois and his wife Margaret, dated 1300. Sir Roger's head rests rather gruesomely on the body of a Saracen, and his feet on his faithful hound.

His local guide told Sampson the legendary tale that on

August 2nd each year the two Crusaders rise from their tombs and together take a walk at dead of night down to Stalham Broad. He added that a woman he knew had once encountered the knights when she was coming home late, and the shock caused a stroke. 'These tombs have been watched heaps of times,' he said, describing to his fascinated listener how the two effigies were seen to leave the church together and go down to the water and then return again to take their places beside their wives.

The possibility of witnessing this incredible event was something Charles Sampson, with his great interest in supernatural tales of the Broads, could not resist, and several well-known gentlemen of the time (pre Second World War) accompanied him on the following August 1st to eagerly await the following night's happening.

They went to the church that afternoon and one of the party was busy finding the best position to erect his camera, but after taking three pictures the camera tripod suddenly fell over when no one was standing anywhere near it. There seemed nothing to account for how such a heavy piece of equipment could have tipped over by itself.

On the next night Sampson and his friends waited impatiently for midnight, keeping as still and silent as they could. The church was cold and eerie, and the time of waiting seemed interminable, but suddenly they were aware of a distinct icy cold breeze passing through the nave and then the sound of a crack. Impossible as it seemed they could see the figure of Sir Oliver de Ingham sit up on his tomb, throw his legs over the side, and stand up, now clad not in dusty stone but in shining armour, a tall, striking figure looking expectantly towards the tomb of Sir Roger de Bois. Then came another loud crack, and

Sir Oliver walked over to the tomb where Sir Roger too sat up and joined him and together they walked to the main door, opened it and walked out into the night.

Sampson and his stunned companions, one using a movie camera, followed the two knights down to the Broad, and at the water's edge, out of nowhere, they saw an Eastern looking soldier spring forward and attack the knights with his scimitar. They fought ferociously until Sir Roger managed to grasp the enemy round the throat, forcibly choking him until his struggles finally subsided and his body was flung into the reeds. Was this perhaps the same Saracen whose body lies beneath Sir Roger's effigy?

The onlookers then saw the two knights return to the church and go inside, where they knelt before the altar and then resumed their former positions by their wives, once more lifeless stone figures.

It must have seemed like a dream, but Sampson and his friends still had the pictures they had taken to develop. The strangest proved to be the one which appeared on the plate which had been in the camera when it fell over on that first afternoon. It showed a cloudy area in one corner in which could be seen a face, the face of Sir Oliver de Ingham! They also had photographic evidence of the empty places on the tombs after the knights had left. Charles Sampson is rather vague about what the movie camera captured, just remarking that 'considering all things' they turned out well.

Charles Sampson's *Ghosts of the Broads* is full of paranormal tales of the area, some legendary stories handed down by word of mouth, and some a matter of historical research. Did he and his friends actually witness this strange event he described so graphically? The companions he mentioned were men of such consequence in their world that it seems unlikely they would have allowed their names to be associated with nothing more than a fanciful fictional ghost story.

As Sampson says, such apparitions are not perceptible to everybody, but perhaps one August night, if you or I should happen to be coming home late along the road that leads to Holy Trinity church, we might see two tall figures clanking along, the moonlight shining strangely on ancient armour as Sir Oliver and Sir Roger set off to keep their legendary rendezvous with a Saracen enemy who never wins the battle.

17

Ghostly Bookworms

FELBRIGG HALL, for centuries the home of the Windham family, is now National Trust property. When I visited the Hall in the summer of 1999 my main interest was to see the library, said to be haunted by William Windham III, and I found it had a suitably dim and ghostly atmosphere. It was easy to imagine that a man who loved books as much as he did would be happy to return to browse peacefully among the beautifully bound volumes.

Windham's pride and joy were the books which had once belonged to his friend Dr Samuel Johnson. He visited the great man during his last illness and inherited Johnson's own copies of the *Iliad, Odyssey* and *New Testament,* and he bought 18 other volumes at a sale of Johnson's effects in 1788.

It is these treasured books that the ghost of William Windham has returned to browse among and where he has been seen from time to time.

When I visited Blickling Hall I met David Musson in the secondhand bookshop there, and found that he had worked for many years as Administrator at Felbrigg Hall and had actually encountered William Windham's ghost – although he insisted that he still didn't really believe in such things!

'It was about 28 years ago,' he told me. 'It was in November, in the late afternoon, and just as it was getting dark I went into the library and noticed that there was a gentleman sitting by the fire reading a book. I thought nothing of it, but then realised that there was no one else in the building but me at that time. After a few seconds he closed the book and put it on the table beside him, and just faded away.

'Later when I told the old butler about it he said, "Yes, that's William Windham. He comes to look at the Samuel Johnson books. We always leave them out for him." '

Mr Musson said that the ghost has been seen again, but not since about 1990. Someone who went into the library to put up the shutters saw William Windham sitting there.

After the Windhams, the house passed into the hands of the Kitton family, and one of them told the author Augustus Hare: 'Mr Windham comes every night to look after his favourite books in the library. He goes straight to the shelves where they are; we hear him moving the tables and chairs about. We never disturb him though, for we intend to be ghosts ourselves some day and to come about the place just as he does.'

Small wonder that William Windham still loves his library as books meant a great deal to him. In fact, he met his death through his attempt to save a friend's large and valuable library one night when he saw a neighbouring house on fire and feared it would soon spread. Knowing his friend was away he got bystanders to help him rescue most of the books, but while carrying out some heavy volumes he slipped, and fell, bruising his hip. Some time later as a result of that injury he underwent a serious operation but unfortunately did not recover.

The 15th century Mannington Hall with its beautiful gardens also has a story of a gentle, bookish apparition and we have a full description from the Rev Dr Jessop who came there to visit Lord Orford on 10th October 1879.

In his account in *The Athenaeum* of January 1880 Dr Jessop tells us that the purpose of his visit to Mannington Hall was to consult certain rare books in the library. The other guests went off to bed at about 10.30 pm, leaving Dr Jessop to work by the light of four candles beside a cosy fire.

At about 1 am, his work almost done, he paused for a drink of seltzer water, and had almost finished with the last volume when he suddenly noticed a large white hand within a foot of his elbow.

'Turning my head, there sat the figure of a somewhat large man with his back to the fire, bending slightly over the table and apparently examining the pile of books that I had been at work upon. The man's face was turned away from me, but I saw his closely cut reddish brown hair, his ear and shaven cheek, the eyebrow, the corner of the right eye, the side of the forehead, and the large high cheek-bone. He was dressed in what I can only describe as a kind of ecclesiastical habit of thick corded silk, or some such material, close up to the throat, and a narrow rim or edging of about an inch broad, of satin or velvet, serving as a stand-up collar and fitting close to the chin. The right hand, which had first attracted my attention, was clasping, without any great pressure, the left hand; both hands were in perfect repose and the large blue veins of the left hand were conspicuous. I remember thinking that the hand was like the hand of Velasquez' magnificent *Dead Knight* in the National Gallery.

'I looked at my visitor for some seconds and was perfectly sure he was not a reality. A thousand thoughts came crowding upon me, but not the least feeling of alarm, or even uneasiness: curiosity and a strong interest were uppermost. For an instant I felt eager to make a sketch of my friend and I looked at a tray on my right for a pencil; then I thought "Upstairs I have a sketch book, shall I fetch it?" There he sat and I was fascinated: afraid, not of his staying, but lest he should go.

'Stopping in my writing, I lifted my right hand from the paper, stretched it out to the pile of books and moved the top one. I cannot explain why I did this – my arm passed in front of the figure and it vanished. I was simply disappointed and nothing more. I went on with my writing as if nothing had happened, perhaps for another five minutes, and had actually got to the last few words of what I had determined to extract when the figure appeared again, exactly in the same place and attitude as before. I saw the hands close to my own; I turned my head to examine him more closely, and I was framing a sentence to address him when I discovered that I did not dare to speak. I was afraid of the sound of my own voice. There he sat and there sat I.

'I turned my head again to my work and finished writing the two or three words I still had to write. The paper and my notes are at this moment before me and exhibit not the slightest tremor or nervousness . . . Having finished my task I shut the book and threw it on the table; it made a slight noise as it fell – the figure vanished.'

Dr Jessop sat for a short time, wondering if his visitor would return, then he put back the books except for the one he had been using when the phantom appeared. Then he blew out the candles, and went off to bed where he slept soundly.

'And this is the conclusion of the story,' he finished, 'but whether hallucination, spectral illusion, or trickery, no one has been able to prove, and as the hero of the tale declines to proffer explanation, theory or inference, the affair continues to be a mystery.'

Apparently a steward afterwards suggested that Dr Jessop's ghost was actually a servant who came in to remove the brandy bottle, but Dr Jessop insisted that he had only drunk seltzer. And beside the fact that the doctor's detailed description of appearance and behaviour hardly seems to fit a servant, surely it would have been quite simple to check whether any member of the staff resembled Dr Jessop's midnight caller.

But since this Mannington ghost seems to have made no other appearance, a mystery it must remain.

18

The Curious Case of the Egyptian Princess's Mummy

To many people the words 'Egyptian mummy' conjure up memories of old Hollywood films with Boris Karloff at his terrifying best, swathed in crumbling bandages and bent on evil. And of course, there was always said to be a curse on anyone who vandalised the tombs of long dead pharoahs, which gained extra credence on the mysterious death of Lord Carnarvon after his discovery of the amazing tomb of Tutankhamun, and the various other disasters associated with the so called curse of the boy King.

One of the most famous stories concerned the haunted mummy case in the British Museum, said to have belonged to a high princess of Amon-Ra whose burial chamber had contained a curse against any who despoiled her resting place. Apparently an Egyptologist was offered the beautiful case, decorated in enamel and gold, by a disreputable American in Cairo in 1910. He couldn't resist such an opportunity but not long afterwards heard that the American had died mysteriously shortly after leaving him, and later another Egyptologist enlightened him about the curse. He laughed at such superstition, but a few days later on a shooting expedition he accidentally shot his own hand, and damaged it so seriously that later his arm had to be amputated.

Then two Egyptian servants who had handled the mummy case died within the year, and when the owner arrived home and looked at the case, the face in his own words 'seemed to come alive with a stare that chilled the blood'. He decided to get rid of it, but a woman friend pleaded with him to let her have it, and within weeks her mother died, her lover left her and she became seriously ill with a mysterious disease. The case was returned to its previous owner, but by now too terrified to own it he presented it to the British Museum. But this was not the end of its alarming history.

A photographer took some pictures of it and promptly dropped dead, and an Egyptologist in charge of the exhibit was found dead at home. A New York museum agreed to accept it, insisting that there should be no publicity about the already notorious mummy case, and it was arranged to send it on the maiden voyage of a superb new liner leaving from Southampton. Everyone knows what happened when on 15th April 1912 the 'unsinkable' boat sank after colliding with an iceberg and hundreds of its passengers were lost. The vessel's name was of course, the *Titanic.*

This is just one of many 'Mummy's Curse' stories, but the ghost of a centuries old Egyptian Princess managed to create something of a stir much nearer home, in Great Yarmouth.

Until it moved quite recently, the St Nicholas (Priory) Junior School occupied a building which dates back more than 700 years to the time when it was a Benedictine priory that played an important role in the history of the town. Towards the end of the 16th century, however, the buildings were in a ruinous condition and they steadily deteriorated as time went on. It was in 1845 that a terrible disaster happened in Yarmouth which proved to be the catalyst for a complete change in the life of the old priory. It would obviously have caused interest and amusement among local people when the clown from a circus in the area announced his intention of sailing up the river Bure in a wash-tub, drawn by four geese. A crowd gathered on the suspension bridge over the river to watch, and as the clown and his geese approached, everybody rushed to one side of the bridge to see him sail beneath. Under the pressure of so many people a defective bar gave way, the chains snapped and the crowd were precipitated straight into the water. The result was chaos, as the mass of people struggled for their lives. Fortunately many were rescued, but 79, mainly children and young lads, were drowned.

It was a great tragedy and the Rev Henry Mackenzie, then minister of the parish, took the opportunity of directing public attention to the want of education among the poorer classes. Subsequently it was suggested that the remains of the priory should be restored and converted to the use of a National School, and eventually in 1853 the Priory School was opened.

A dramatised history entitled *From Priory to School* was enacted by the pupils in 1973 and a booklet issued at the same time told the story of this ancient building. Mr Harold Taylor who was the Headmaster at that time kindly gave me a copy of this booklet which includes the fascinating account of the Egyptian Princess's mummy. He thinks these extraordinary happenings occurred around 1920, or maybe a bit earlier.

Apparently a 19th century addition to the original old building was used as a museum and some of the exhibits probably stood in the recesses around the room. It is easy to imagine that a real Egyptian mummy case would have had pride of place and it would have been interesting to know its origin, but I have been unable to trace just how this unusual object came into the possession of the school.

However, although the mysterious mummy has long gone, Mr Taylor told me that when he was at the school none of his school cleaners were happy to carry out their duties in that room by themselves; they all felt there was an unnatural chill in the atmosphere and an unpleasant feel to the place.

The curious tale of the Egyptian Princess's mummy begins when an unpleasant smell began to be noticed in what was called the Commercial Room. It became so bad that something had to be done as it seemed likely that a rat had died beneath the floorboards. They were ripped up but no rodent was found nor anything to account for the smell. However, someone's keen nose led them to the mummy case and, no doubt with some misgiving, it was opened.

The case contained a mummy, and the source of the smell had been found, as due possibly to damp the mummy had rotted and obviously needed to be disposed of urgently. It was decided to bury the remains in the nearby churchyard of St Nicholas's church, but someone insisted that according to ancient custom one could not bury a mummified princess in daylight, this must be carried out at midnight!

The subsequent midnight scene was worthy of a Hammer Horror film. A small burial party assembled at the witching hour and, secretly entering the school by a back entrance, they collected the mummy, duly buried it in the graveyard and thankfully returned the case to the school.

It was a few weeks later that the family in the nearby vicarage were woken in the night. Someone was knocking at the door, but when the door was opened, there was no one outside. The same thing happened the next night, and again no one was there. Then some time later, a party of workmen passing through the churchyard heard tapping on the church door. Thinking that someone had been locked inside they fetched the keys and opened the door, but no one was waiting inside, and a thorough search showed the church to be quite empty.

It was a mystery, especially as soon afterwards the knocking on the vicarage door recommenced. When yet again no one was found to account for it, the police were called in case some mischief maker was responsible, but no one was caught and the tapping had started up again inside the church.

By now local gossip had decided that a ghost was abroad, obviously the restless ghost of the Egyptian Princess, and such large crowds gathered outside the churchyard railings, hoping for a sighting, that in the end the police had to put a cordon round the graveyard.

As if this wasn't enough, the same unpleasant smell had returned to the room where the mummy case was kept. Yet again the case was opened and one can imagine the horrified feelings of the staff when inside they found the remains of the mummy's leg! Obviously in a combination of secrecy, hurry and darkness the burial party had unfortunately broken off the leg and left it behind. There was no alternative but to inter the leg with the rest of the mummy's remains, and that apparently was the end of the knockings in the night, and the Egyptian Princess was finally at rest.

There was a rather macabre suggestion that the Princess had not been able to rest minus one leg, and so had hopped about on the other looking for it, thus causing the apparent tapping noises! But the idea of a mummy on the hop is too undignified – I'm sure Boris Karloff would have thought so!

19

Will o' the Wisps, Black Dogs and Other Mysteries

IN THE graveyard at Thurlton, north of Beccles, lies Joseph Bexfield who met his end on 11th August 1809 in the marshes. He wanted to cross the marsh to Thurlton Staithe on a night when the Jack o' Lanterns or Will o' the Wisps were dancing and flickering all over the place, but despite warnings of the danger, Joseph set off, confident that an experienced old fenman like himself was safe enough. And that was the last anyone saw of him until his body was washed up later.

It's said he can sometimes be seen standing on his gravestone telling passers-by how he was lured to his death by a Will o' the Wisp and drowned when he fell into a dyke. In the days before the fens were drained, these strange lights that bobbed and danced in all directions caused great fear in marshland areas as although it was known that they were caused by a spontaneous combustion of marsh gas, they did seem to have a life of their own and would appear to follow people and often behave in a mischievous or even malevolent manner.

Certainly to many Fenland people the 'Lantern Man' as

they called it was seen as some kind of spirit. In an article in the *Eastern Counties Magazine* in 1900, Lady Cranworth of Letton wrote that an old local man told her that if two men stood at opposite ends of a field and whistled, the Lantern Man would always run towards the whistle. People believed that if anyone ran away from the Lantern Man he would always run after them and the advice was: 'If the Lantern Man light upon you, the best thing is to throw yourself flat on your face and hold your breath.' This was no doubt to avoid breathing in the marsh gas but it was a common belief that the 'Shiners' as they were also known in the Breckland area were something to fear.

In *Norfolk Broads and Rivers,* Christopher Davies quotes an old wherryman as saying he always fired his gun at them to put them out, 'for if you did not fire at them, they were likely to come near you and do you some hurt'. If someone on horseback encountered a Shiner there was always the danger that the horse would shy and throw the rider.

Mrs Lubbock, the Wise Woman of Irstead, certainly regarded the Jack o' Lantern or Lantern Man as a ghost associated with a man called Heard who had drowned on the Neatishead side of Alderfen Broad, at a place called Heard's Holde. She insisted she had frequently seen him 'rising up and falling and twistering about' and if anyone came along with a lantern and did not put out the light, he would dash it to pieces.

Although after the fens were drained these tantalising lights were seldom seen, it was not the end of the dangers awaiting travellers on lonely roads late at night. Throughout East Anglia there are tales of the Black Dog, Old Shuck or the Galleytrot, a centuries old creature said to be of Norse origin, the black Hound of Odin, which arrived with the Vikings.

Huge, shaggy and black with eyes glowing like hot coals, he revels in stormy weather when his bloodcurdling howl rivals the sound of the wind as he travels coastal paths. To meet Shuck is said to be an omen of death or disaster, but many have lived to tell the tale. It's said that if you sense that Shuck is padding silently behind you, keep walking. On no account run or even turn round to look or, they say, he will growl and snarl like a mad dog, and may attack you with dire results.

There have been several sightings on the old green lane known as Peddars Way. In October 1977 a man walking along near Massingham Heath saw a huge black dog approaching, its jaws wide open showing its frightening teeth. It was obviously unfriendly and when it reached him, it leapt up at him and, terrified, he raised his arm to ward it off. He had closed his eyes but to his amazement nothing happened and when he looked, the dog had disappeared. However, the old superstition that the dog is a creature of ill omen proved to have some substance, as a year to the day later, the man was involved in a serious road accident.

Where Peddars Way crosses the A11 at Roudham Cross a motorist driving along early one morning in 1962 had to brake suddenly when a large black dog began to cross the road in front of him. It seemed impossible to miss it but before he could draw up he saw that the dog was now on the other side of his car, padding along on the Way as if it had passed straight through his vehicle.

Coltishall Bridge near Norwich is one of Shuck's haunts where he is said to appear headless, and the coastal area between Overstrand and Runton is Black Shuck country, especially the former Shucks Lane, definitely a place to avoid if you didn't want to meet him. In some areas he was reputed to have only one eye, set in the middle of his head, and at Sheringham, although he was said to be headless, yet he was described as having great saucer eyes and a white handkerchief tied over the place where his head should have been.

J. Wentworth Day recalls a Norfolk lady's story in his *Ghosts and Witches.* She lived at Hempnall near Norwich, and told him that one night her son came in looking shocked and frightened. She thought he was ill but he told her that coming down a road called Market Hole he had seen what appeared to be a big dog about to cross in front of his bike and had been afraid he would be thrown off, but it just vanished. 'When I got off my bike and looked round, there was nothing to be seen, and I felt awful,' he said.

In his *Ghost Book,* Alasdair Alpin MacGregor includes an account of a local man's encounter with the Black Dog. He was on his way home after an evening with friends at Bungay en route to Ditchingham station. He noticed a black object approaching and as it got nearer he could see it was a large black dog with a long shaggy coat. It was on the same side of the road as himself, so he moved into the centre of the road to let it pass, but when it came level with him, it vanished! He stopped and looked behind and also over the hedge to see if it had gone into the meadow, but there was no sign of the creature and, suddenly afraid, he hurried off home. His friends told him he had met Black Shuck which everybody around there knew about, and some had seen.

In John Harries' *Ghost Hunters Road Book* (1968) he says

that the A149 between Hunstanton and Cromer is one of Shuck's favourite haunts where paths run along the cliff tops. For anyone brave enough to risk an encounter with the legendary beast, he recommends taking the path from Cromer lighthouse to Overstrand.

It's believed that Black Shuck was Conan Doyle's inspiration for the book *The Hound of the Baskervilles.* He came to Cromer in 1905 with his friend Fletcher Robinson for a golfing holiday, and in his own words 'one raw Sunday afternoon when the wind rushed off the North Sea', Robinson, inspired perhaps by the stormy weather, began telling his companion about spectral dogs. It's said that one of the hotel waiters told Conan Doyle that his father had actually encountered Black Shuck running along the beach and, with his fascination with the supernatural, the famous writer must have seen the potential for a good story.

Fletcher Robinson was a Devon man, and would no doubt have also told his friend about Dartmoor's own terrifying pack of Whist hounds or Yeth hounds, and perhaps also the Black Dog of Torrington. Add the fact that a coachman who worked for the Robinson family in Devon was called Baskerville and it is easy to guess how it was that Conan Doyle's imagination had soon produced his famous detective novel.

For some who experience sightings of the legendary black dog, it is merely an uncanny incident such as the coastguard on duty at Gorleston Rescue headquarters one morning who saw a large hound-type black dog running along the beach. He noticed it because it kept stopping as if searching for someone, but then it vanished before his eyes. It was quite a shock as the beach was flat with nowhere the dog could have gone. The man had never heard of Black Shuck until he mentioned the experience to colleagues and one from Cromer enlightened him.

But for writer Christopher Marlowe, his encounter with the legendary creature was a nightmare. He had heard that a man had been savagely attacked by Shuck in a lane leading down to the marshes from the Wells-Stiffkey road, and he bravely – or foolishly – decided to lie in wait one night in the hope of seeing the black dog.

Without explaining what he meant to do, he arranged to stay the night at a nearby cottage, and set off for the spot armed with a torch and a heavy stick, and a warning from the cottage owner not to venture on the marsh after dark. As time went by he began to question his own foolhardiness, and wonder, if he too was attacked, whether he could make it to the cottage in time. It was a long wait, but at last from his hiding place near a pool he could discern a distant shadow approaching. But suddenly he heard the most appalling howl – 'it froze the blood in my veins and caused my hair to stand right on end,' he said.

Even worse, the shadow was turning into a huge black hound which was obviously on its way to the pool where he was hiding, and appeared to be on the trail of something or somebody!

Marlowe didn't wait any longer; he jumped up and fled towards the cottage, not daring to look back. Stumbling and out of breath, he raced up the path and hammered on the door, shouting for the owner to come quickly. Thankfully he saw a light approaching and as the door was unbolted, he took one frightened glance back and saw 'a pair of ferocious eyes' right behind him. He fell fainting into the cottage as the door opened and was slammed shut as a heavy body seemed to leap through the air and thud down on to the ground outside. He was safe, but as he said, 'it was long before I could sleep.'

Spectral black dogs are known throughout the whole country under a variety of names but in part of Norfolk they have their own version of Black Shuck's origin. There was a terrific storm in January 1709 when the sea off the coast between Blakeney and Mundesley swept over the beaches and across the marshes, causing damage everywhere. A boat caught in the storm was carried helplessly towards the shore at Salthouse as the gales and high seas broke it apart. The crew had no chance, but the Captain clutched the collar of his pet wolfhound and the two plunged into the water in a desperate bid to save themselves. The currents proved too strong, however, and their bodies were found, the Captain still grasping the dog's collar and the dog's jaws clamped onto his master's jacket. The crew and Captain were buried in Salthouse churchyard, and the wolfhound was buried in the beach.

They say that within weeks people noticed a big black dog running backwards and forwards on the beach between Cley and Salthouse, howling for his master. That was nearly 300 years ago and any more recent sightings of a black dog thereabouts describe him as big as a calf, with eyes glowing red as coals and a long, black shaggy coat. Black Shuck or not, when the wind howls on wild stormy winter nights, the marshes between Salthouse and Cley are no place for a walk!

20

The Maddermarket Ghost

'MOST THEATRES worthy of the name have a ghost,' declared Mr Nugent Monck at one of his famous lectures. And he had reason to know because his charming small Maddermarket Theatre in Norwich was reputed to be haunted by the shadowy figure of a priest, seen in the old Georgian building long before Mr Monck acquired it in 1921 as home for his Norwich Players.

The building had had a varied career as a Roman Catholic church, a Salvation Army hall and a baking powder factory, before Nugent Monck saw its potential and transformed it into an Elizabethan style theatre with a gallery and apron stage where his company could perform Shakespeare's plays in an ideal setting.

It was not long afterwards that the building's resident apparition made an appearance. During a Saturday matinee, Peter Taylor Smith who was prompting was surprised to see a priest standing nearby, apparently surveying the audience, and then suddenly he wasn't there. It was no illusion, as a Roman Catholic priest chanced to be in the audience that afternoon, and he too noticed the figure.

And in his case it was not the first time this had happened. Some years before, he had been in the building and had seen the identical figure apparently kneeling in prayer, only to vanish suddenly in the same way.

Although Mr Monck insisted that he didn't believe in such things as ghosts, he declared that he had a great capacity for seeing them, and enjoyed regaling his listeners with stories of his theatre's own apparition.

As the theatre was once a Roman Catholic church, perhaps it is not unexpected that its ghost should be a priest, and local legend had it that he was returning to complete a mass which was interrupted many years ago.

Mr Monck once saw the apparition cross from the place where a confessional box used to stand to the site of another on the other side of the theatre. And on another occasion when he entered the theatre without putting on the lights, he was enveloped in 'something ghastly cold' as he stood by the confessional boxes.

But Nugent Monck was obviously a man of strong nerves. He was not afraid to sleep in the theatre, which he often did during wartime, although he admitted that he sometimes experienced an uneasy feeling that he was being watched when he was alone in the building.

His home too, in Ninham's Court, once an old dilapidated building which he had lovingly restored, was apparently shared with some of those ghosts he didn't believe in!

He airily claimed that one was someone who had hanged himself from a beam. 'I have been lying in bed and his toes have tickled my nose,' he declared, and some guests visiting his house also witnessed this alarming spectacle. Some of his pet cats too were noticeably reluctant to pass a certain spot on the way to the bathroom, but others were seen to be apparently rubbing themselves affectionately against the legs of an unseen presence.

One day the stage manager, Pat Bullen, was going up to the light box at the back of the theatre when he noticed a figure in what appeared to be a black cloak, climbing the ladder ahead of him. He followed on, but when he reached the box there was no one there, and no other way out.

Mr Bullen, like his employer, stoutly insisted that he didn't believe in ghosts, but he did concede that although the theatre usually felt as normal as anywhere else, there were times when there was a really strange atmosphere there.

Another member of staff, Percy Ayres, was doing some wiring under the stage one day when he heard someone walking on the boards above his head. He needed some help with his work so he called to whoever it was to come down and give him a hand. But there was no response to his calls, and when he crawled out to see why, he found there was no one else in the theatre.

Unexplained smells are sometimes associated with hauntings, and Lionel Dunn, who often used to go into the theatre on Sunday mornings, frequently noticed a distinct smell of incense, and he – and other people – experienced the creepy sensation that they were being watched by some invisible presence.

But ghostly sightings, smells, sounds and eerie sensations now seem to belong to the theatre's past. Perhaps the Maddermarket Theatre's ghostly priest has finally abandoned his unfinished mass and passed on. Or perhaps that gentleman in clerical garb sitting near you in the stalls is not quite what he seems?

21

Bircham Newton

THERE WERE many airfields throughout East Anglia during the Second World War from which RAF and USAAF bombers and fighter planes flew the Channel on their dangerous missions, and perhaps it is not surprising that so much courage and camaraderie coupled with tragedy and loss has left more than memories.

Many of these former wartime airfields have a history of strange happenings – the sound of a plane in an empty sky, a man in uniform who casually walks through a solid wall, or who hitches a lift, only to vanish en route.

Perhaps the best known of these airfields is Bircham Newton, originally built in 1914 and now home to the National Construction College. In 1970 a film crew were there making a management training film and, while they were working, without warning a heavy studio lamp suddenly fell towards Peter Clark, one of the crew, who was standing directly underneath. Luckily for him, just as it was about to hit him it swerved away, just as if it had been diverted by an unseen hand! No one apparently thought much of this at the time, but even stranger things were to follow.

Later, Kevin Garry, another member of the crew,

discovered that there were two squash courts at Bircham, and he borrowed a raquet and ball to play, but none of the others wanted to join him so off he went, having borrowed the only key to the building. At first he practised in the left hand court, and then tried the right hand one, and while he was playing he heard footsteps coming along the viewing gallery behind him. He simply assumed that one of the crew had decided to join him after all, then remembered that the door was locked and he had the key. At that moment he heard a sigh which made the hairs on the back of his neck prickle, and when he looked round, there in the gallery watching him was a man in RAF uniform. And as he looked, the figure vanished! Kevin wasted no more time – he fled.

When Peter Clark heard what had happened he suggested they take a tape recorder to the courts to see if it recorded anything. 'It was a warm moonlit night when we returned to the courts,' said Peter. 'We visited the left hand court which felt completely normal, but when we went into the court on the right the atmosphere was so cold, so frightening that it was like stepping into another world.'

The two men left the tape running and waited outside. They had locked the door, and were able to see that no one else got into the building. As they collected the tape just as it was coming to the end, they heard footsteps coming along the gallery. They came nearer but there was no one to be seen, and the frightened men grabbed the recorder and ran.

Many people, including myself, have heard this tape which sounds as if it comes from a large, echoing building, perhaps a hangar. There are metallic sounds, muffled speech and a woman's voice, but what she is saying is impossible to identify. The sound of a piston-engined aircraft can be heard, and finally there is a really strange loud noise. The tape used was brand new, so there was no question of previous recordings being on it, and exterior sounds could not have penetrated the nine inch brick walls of the courts. In any case, it was near midnight on a calm, quiet night.

Later Peter Clark returned to the airfield with a medium, who as soon as he entered the squash courts made contact with a dead airman. On the tape the medium can be heard asking, 'What is your name?' And finally the answer came – 'Wiley'. Clark discovered in local newspaper files that an airman called Wiley had committed suicide at the airfield in World War Two.

Enquiries revealed that the airfield had had a reputation for being haunted for a long time. A student on a construction course had his bedclothes pulled off at night by an unseen hand, another found his curtains torn down and thrown across the room, radiators in the officers' mess were always being turned off, and one student left hurriedly after seeing a figure in RAF uniform walk straight through a solid wall. Some of the recordings were broadcast on the BBC and several listeners who had been stationed at Bircham Newton during the last war wrote in to say that it was common knowledge that the ghost of an airman was frequently seen about the place. It was also considered to be an unlucky airfield. In the early part of the war after the American Air Force moved in, on one occasion they despatched 13 bombers on a raid from which not one returned.

A BBC TV team took two leading spiritualists to the

airfield, taking care not to tell them anything about previous happenings. They both immediately sensed the spirit of a dead airman in the squash courts, and the famous medium John Sutton commented that there was a lot of psychic power being generated in the building.

John Sutton went into a trance and began to speak in a sort of hoarse whisper, the voice of an airman called Dusty Miller, who had been killed in a crash with his friends Pat Sullivan and Gerry Arnold when their plane came down in flames behind a church. When Sutton came out of his trance he said that the three airmen had been keen squash players and had made a pact that if anything happened to them they would try to meet again in the building.

'Very often people don't realise what has happened when they die,' he said. 'Their sense of time is quite different and these three airmen were earthbound because they didn't realise they were dead. They desperately needed help.' He had told them that they must let go of the earth, look up and go towards the light.

Later, records were checked and it was found that an RAF Anson plane had crashed behind Bircham church killing the crew of three.

By coincidence, the BBC sent a woman reporter, Rita Dando, to Bircham Newton, and she arrived with a woman friend later the same day. They borrowed the key to the squash courts and locked themselves in, but the locked door flew open and then slammed shut three times. They knew there was no one else in the building and they had the only key. Then their tape recorder refused to function, so they returned to their hotel where they found that the tape recorder was now working perfectly.

So are the ghostly happenings at Bircham Newton all in the past? While I was researching this book a film crew were at the airfield making a television film for a Japanese TV programme whose viewers are apparently fascinated by the paranormal. Apparently they found the atmosphere in the squash courts unnaturally icy, and although there was no breeze, the door slammed suddenly.

But despite no ghost taking part in their programme, the Anglia Society for Paranormal Research, who have been visiting the airfield regularly for the past ten years, were able to supply evidence that Bircham Newton's haunting reputation is well earned. 'The place is very haunted, not just the squash court but two or three other buildings,' Keith Webster, the Society's technical co-ordinator, told me.

They have come to the conclusion that the entities which haunt the squash court are two men and a woman and have based this on the voices heard. They leave their micro-transmitter on the wall inside while they remain outside with their tape recorder, and it is only afterwards when they play back the tape that they can hear the voices interacting with their own. Sometimes they have heard the ghosts taking their transmitter apart and reassembling it, and once they heard the woman's voice say 'Pack it in you two'. They know that the entities are aware of their presence as they have actually heard them refer to his fellow member Wendy Hudson by name!

They have formed the opinion that when the plane crashed killing the three airmen who haunted the squash court, there was an unauthorised WRAF Officer on the plane, probably the girlfriend of one of the men.

The group from the Anglia Society for Paranormal

Research have taken photographs which show swirling mist like a vortex but another shows shapes which can be discerned as those of a man and a woman together, and Keith Webster thinks that the squash courts may have been used for a romantic rendezvous.

Recordings have also produced loud noises and knocking, footsteps and whistling and occasionally voices. Are some of these sounds some kind of playback from those wartime days so long ago?

The ghosts in the squash courts seem more like actual entities but, I wondered, are they always there, earth-bound, or do they come and go? Keith Webster said he thinks they come and go. 'We see strange lights sometimes like a beam or a spotlight which could possibly be the entrance to a parallel universe.'

Someone who served as a WAAF at the airfield during the last war recalled that often fellow WAAFs on night duty reported hearing a car race along and crash into the wall of a hangar, but when they rushed out to help the driver, there was nothing to be seen. Another story relates to a phantom sports car full of laughing airmen which races across the base to crash into the back of a hangar. Surely it must be the same one? Nearly sixty years later, are the ghosts of those brave young airmen still living their war? Still forgetting tomorrow's rendezvous with danger in a night out with their mates, or a romantic liaison with a lover? The medium John Sutton told the three in the squash court to leave the earth behind and go towards the light. Let's hope some day this will happen.

22

Ghosts Galore

Isabella's Laughter

THEY SAY that Castle Rising once had a busy seaport, but now the sea is four miles away from the castle, which although ruined must once have been fit for a Queen. But the Queen who lived here – Isabella – died quite mad because of the loneliness and isolation.

Isabella was a beautiful French princess, married to Edward II who neglected her for his favourite, Piers Gaveston, and his relationship caused opposition among his barons, one of whom, Roger Mortimer, formed a liaison with Isabella. Eventually the King was deposed in 1327 in favour of his 14 year old son, Edward III, but attempts to rescue him signed his death warrant as Mortimer gave orders that he was to be murdered.

To the young King, already uneasy at Mortimer's growing power, his father's death was a deciding factor, and one night a party of his men invaded Nottingham Castle where Mortimer and Isabella were, and arrested him. The Queen's screams as she pleaded for her lover's life were of no avail and he was convicted of the King's murder and hanged at Tyburn in 1330. Isabella was banished to Castle Rising, but although her son decreed that she should never show her face in public again she was allowed a suitable entourage of knights and ladies to keep her company.

However, after her dramatic life of power and excitement, the isolation of Castle Rising must have been far from her taste, and the occasional state visits of her son would merely have emphasised what she was missing. Isabella lived mostly at Castle Riding until her death 27 years later, finally becoming demented. It is said that her shrieks and manic laughter can still be heard above the howling wind on that stormy coast.

The Body in the Flag

The Romans built Burgh Castle as one of their Forts of the Saxon Shore, and it still remains as a substantial ruin three miles west of Great Yarmouth. It has a ghostly mystery to which no one seems to have the answer.

Who was the unfortunate victim whose body, wrapped in a white flag, is flung, or perhaps jumps, down from the ruins to the foreshore?

It is said to happen every year on 3rd July.

Cromwell in Love

In Rosalind Heywood's book *The Infinite Hive* (1964) she mentions the Norfolk home of an aunt which was haunted. As a child Rosalind was conscious of invisible presences which frightened her, but after she was grown-up she realised that her aunt was well aware of them, and in fact could see them, but took them for granted. One day her aunt was lunching with friends and saw a portrait of a man in 17th century clothes. 'Why,' she cried, 'that's the man who is always trying to stop me going upstairs at home.'

'That', said her host, 'was Oliver Cromwell as a young man. As it happens when he was young he was involved in an unfortunate love affair with a girl who lived in your house.'

Ghosts in the Cathedral Close

It is well known that building work can sometimes stir up paranormal activity in ancient premises, and this was the case in the Cathedral Close in Norwich when builders were called in to remove an ancient stone slab staircase in the basement of an office. Before long, staff working there were made aware that something decidedly strange was happening as a cupboard door started to bang open and shut of its own accord, repeatedly hammering noisily against a desk. Then a calendar started to swing like a pendulum and the wall clock moved by itself, and remained hanging at an angle, defying gravity. It seemed as if ordinary office equipment was going crazy as paper-clips started jumping in the air, and a hole-punch was suddenly pushed off a shelf when no one was near it.

'After each event there was a horrible presence in the room,' said one secretary, 'it went very cold and there was a fusty smell hanging in the air, like Gauloise cigarettes. We could feel somebody was in the room with us.'

Staff remembered that the room in the basement had always been referred to as the Phantom Room although no one knew why, except that there was a dank, icy chill to the atmosphere down there, and even the builders confessed to feeling uneasy while working in the area. Some members of the staff would never go down alone, and in the light of the poltergeist activity in the offices, it was suggested that perhaps something was buried down there and the builders had unwittingly disturbed it.

The firm decided to call on the help of a deliverance team, a group of Norfolk clergy appointed by the Bishop to deal with exorcism, and where paranormal events are causing disturbance, it is their mission to bring peace and light.

Afterwards the room in the basement which had appeared to be the focus of the haunting was used as a storeroom. But what was its history, and why was it known as the Phantom Room? A spokeswoman for the Cathedral said at the time: 'The Close has had a turbulent and sometimes violent history and there are many things we don't know about its past. It would not be beyond the bounds of possibility if there had been a violent act or a tragedy on that spot.'

Owd Sir Berney

Sir Berney Brograve, known as Owd Sir Berney, is a colourful part of Norfolk folklore. His father bought Waxham, Worstead and Horsey manors in 1733 and the family lived in Waxham Hall, said to be haunted by six ancestors, all of whom had died in battle.

Sir Berney, too, enjoyed a good fight and once after a chimney sweep had swept all the chimneys at the Hall, Sir Berney offered to fight him for the money. If the sweep won he would get double the money, if he lost he would obviously get the worst of it, and no money.

Apparently the sweep lost, but Sir Berney's battering had raised such a cloud of soot that he almost choked and was obliged to drink even more than usual.

Naturally a robust character like Sir Berney Brograve took a few ancestral apparitions for granted, and every

New Year's Eve he entertained them all in fine style. They were Sir Ralph, killed in the Crusades, Sir Edmund in the Baron's Wars, Sir John at Agincourt, Sir Francis in the Wars of the Roses, Sir Thomas at Marston Moor and Sir Charles, killed at Ramillies, and all were invited to dine and drink the night away with their descendant, Sir Berney, until at the stroke of midnight, like Cinderella, they vanished.

Berney's son Sir George, who died in 1828, was the end of the line but the Brograves are never likely to be forgotten. And, like his ancestors, they say Sir Berney is still around and can be seen on wild stormy nights, galloping by between Worstead and Waxham.

Alas, Poor Yorick!

An American actor, Del Close, who died in 1999 bequeathed his skull to Chicago's Goodman Theatre, suggesting in his will that it could be used in *Hamlet* in the scene where the Prince holds up the skull of the old court jester and laments 'Alas, poor Yorick!' The director of the theatre undertook to fulfil the actor's wishes, and find a part for his skull every season when possible!

A rather macabre story you may think, and what has it to do with Norfolk? Well, when I read it in a recent copy of *Fortean Times* I was immediately reminded of something which happened 200 years ago in North Walsham.

It appears that in 1788 at North Walsham theatre, a play called *The Fair Penitent* was being performed. An actress, Mrs Barry, was playing the part of Calista who in the last act is called upon to lay her head upon a skull.

On the occasion in question, as soon as her head touched the skull Mrs Barry felt extremely ill and fell back in a dead faint. She was unable to continue and had to be taken home. But by the next morning she was sufficiently recovered to ask about the skull. 'Where did it come from?' she wanted to know.

'From the sexton,' she was told. 'And whose remains was it?'

'Some actor,' was the answer. 'What was his name?' she pursued.

'Mr Norris.'

Now pale and trembling, Mrs Barry went on, 'Are you sure the name was Norris?'

'Oh, yes,' came the reply, 'He had been buried in St Nicholas's graveyard for twelve years.'

This told poor Mrs Barry what she had feared to hear. In a state of deep shock, she screamed and became so ill that within six weeks she was dead. Mr Norris had been her first husband!

More King's Lynn Ghosts

The town's library was built in 1905 on the site of the graveyard of a Greyfriars monastery. Visits to the basement are not recommended as you may meet the ghost which wears a monk-like habit with the hood drawn over its face.

King's Lynn's oldest town house dating back to 1100 might be expected to have an interesting history, with perhaps a few echoes of the past from time to time. In 1996 the *Eastern Daily Press* reported that the staff at a solicitor's office now occupying premises at King Street had experienced happenings of an unusual and possibly paranormal nature.

One secretary was working late one evening when she

heard footsteps approaching. There was no one else in the office at the time, but she had the uneasy feeling that she was being watched. She looked up and saw the figure of a young man wearing a military style trench coat. She said 'Hello', but there was no reply and the young man promptly vanished!

'I was not frightened at the time as I was so surprised,' she said, 'but it's the last time I shall be working late.'

Another employee agreed that she too had heard unexplained noises when working late, but had not seen the ghost. 'We heard piano playing and noises one night, but when we looked there was nothing there,' she said.

The building has had a variety of uses over the years, and it's thought it was once a tavern so perhaps somehow an echo of pub noises can still be heard at times. But who was the young man in the trench coat?

Great Yarmouth's Whistling Monks

When Yarmouth Fire Brigade moved to their new building in 1972 they soon began to wonder if there might be something a little strange about the place. It was just after midnight one night that one of the men was alone in the dormitory when he heard the sound of whistling coming along the corridor outside. It was a far from cheerful sound, more like a tuneless dirge, which stopped outside the door, but when no one came in, the fireman went to investigate, only to find the corridor empty and no one else about at all! Later another fireman, also alone in the dormitory at the time, heard the sound of someone approaching down the corridor.

'It was a very quick, almost scampering step,' he said, 'like someone half running and half walking.' The footsteps stopped outside the door, but when he looked out, there was no one there.

'It's not the sort of thing you imagine,' he said, 'there was definitely something walking along the corridor.' Naturally it was soon pointed out that the new fire station was built on the site of the 15th century House of Blackfriars, and when the area was excavated a stone coffin and two skeletons had been found.

And a Gorleston woman who had lived in a property on the site as a child, was able to throw further light on the subject. 'People may laugh, but the firemen were not imagining things,' she said. 'I regularly saw monks, misty figures wearing black cloaks with no faces, walking about our house.' These frightening appearances usually happened at about midnight and were preceded by the sound of whistling. Slow footsteps would herald the arrival of monks, and walking with heads bowed and hands clasped inside their cloaks, they would then vanish into the wall.

This lady remembered locked doors being found open and furniture being moved in the night. And her mother had also seen the ghostly figure of an old woman carrying a candle who walked into her bedroom at night and a young girl with long golden hair.

'I believe what the firemen said,' she said, 'because it's true!'

The Guardian Angel at Letheringsett Mill

Have you ever visited Letheringsett Water Mill in North Norfolk?

In 1995 a middle-aged couple approached the table where the proprietor's wife was taking entrance fees and asked for two tickets. 'Did you say two?' she queried, 'I thought the three of you were together.' The couple looked puzzled and she felt foolish when she looked again and saw there were just two of them there. And yet she felt sure a third person, a middle-aged man in a rather shabby grey suit and cloth cap, had been behind them, but now there was no sign of him!

She called her husband who quickly searched the mill, as it is a working mill and dangerous for unescorted visitors. But a search of all four floors revealed no sign of the mystery man, and then someone remembered the ghost!

This is said to be the spirit of a millwright whose job at the mill was to trim the stone grinding wheels, and who now acts as guardian angel, protecting the mill and all who work there from any danger.

Both the owner of the mill and two of his staff recalled that although none of them had actually seen a ghost, they were often aware of an invisible and benign presence. So if you do visit Letheringsett Mill, and you do happen to notice a man in grey wearing an old cloth cap, don't worry if next time you look he seems to have disappeared into thin air. He's just doing his job – looking after things!

Index

Adam and Eve, Norwich 74–75
Alderfen Broad 103
Anglia Society for Paranormal Research 116–117
Aylmerton 66–67
Ayres, Percy 111

Banningham 58
Barnard, Henry 42–46
Barrett, W.H. 34
Barry, Mrs 122–123
Bell, Thetford 25–29
Bexfield, Joseph 102
Bircham Newton 112–117
Birkin, Sir Henry 18
Black dogs 54, 103–108
Black Shuck 54, 73–74, 103–108
Blakeney 108
Blickling Hall 53–56, 83, 91
Bois, Sir Roger de 87–90
Boleyn Anne 7, 53–56, 83
Boleyn, Thomas 53–54
Breckles Hall 83–85
Bridge House pub, Norwich 74
Briston 77
Broads, the 30–33, 35–36, 39, 87–90
Brograve, Sir Berney (Owd Sir Berney) 121–122
Brooke 85
Brown Lady, Raynham Hall 15–20
Bullen, Pat 111
Burgh Castle 73, 119

Caister Castle 83
Castle Rising 118–119
Cawston Heath 54
Chisnell, Dave 64
Clark, Peter 112–114
Cley 108
Cobb Hall, Snettisham 44, 45
Cobb, Robert 43–46
Coltishall Bridge 104
Cranworth, Lady 103
Croasdale, Shaun 79
Cromer 106, 107
Curtiss, Benjamin 32–33

Dando, Rita 115
Davies, Christopher 103
Day, J. Wentworth 7, 105
Day, Margaret 9
Ditchingham 85–86, 105
Doyle, Conan 106
Ducker, Lilian 35–36
Duke's Head Hotel, King's Lynn 10, 11–12, 13
Duke's Head Hotel, Yarmouth 72–73
Dunn, Lionel 111
Durand, Lord Percival 30–32, 33
East Dereham 33–34
Elderton Lodge Hotel, Thorpe Market 76

Felbrigg Hall 91–92
Fenland 33–35, 102–103
Forman, Joan 50–51, 63, 79, 85–86

Galleytrot 103
Garry, Kevin 112–113
Gifford, Alison 13
Globe inn, King's Lynn 12–13
Goodeve, Mrs 40–46
Gorleston 106, 125
Great Melton 81–82
Great Yarmouth 50–52, 72–73, 97–101, 124–125
Grey Ladies 53, 55–56, 75–76

Hall, Bryan 58–61
Hancock, Sidney 56
Happisburgh 37–39
Harries, John 105
Hempnall 105
Heywood, Rosalind 119
Hickling Broad 35–36, 68–69
Hingham 49
Holme Hale 48–49
Horning 70–71
Horsey 121
Houghton Hall 80

Hound of the Baskervilles, The 106
Howat, Polly 67
Hunstanton 106
Hunstanton Hall 21–24, 76
Hunter, Sally 71–72
Hutt, Mary 57–58

Ingham 87–90
Ingham, Sir Oliver de 87–90
Irstead, the Wise Woman of 103
Isabella, Queen 118–119

Jack o' Lanterns 102–103
Jarred, Tony 79
Jessop, Dr Augustus 83, 93–95
John H. Strachey pub, Briston 77

King's Lynn 9–14, 71–72, 123–124

Lang, Andrew 40, 45
Lantern Man, the 102–103
le Strange, Armine (Styleman) 21–24, 76
Letheringsett Mill 125–126
Lodge Hotel, Old Hunstanton 75–76
Lubbock, Mrs, the Wise Woman of Irstead 103

Mace, Jim (George) 84–85
MacGregor, Alasdair Alpin 105
Maddermarket Theatre, Norwich 109–111
Maitland, Rev Rowland W. 40–46
Mannington Hall 83, 93–95
Marlowe, Christopher 107–108
Marryat, Captain 17–18
Massingham Heath 104
Mead, Dennis 54–55
Mitchell, Colin and Maureen 27–28
Monck, Nugent 109–110
Mundesley 108
Musson, David 91–92

Nevill, Lady Dorothy 65–66
North Walsham 122–123
Norwich 62–64, 74–75, 109–111, 120–121

Old Catton 66
Old Ferry Inn, Horning 70–71
Old Hunstanton 75–76
Overstrand 104, 106

Peddars Way 104
Penston Rev Thomas Josiah 32
Potter Heigham 35–36
Prince Christopher of Greece 80
Priory School, Norwich 97–99
Provand, Captain 19
Pump Hill Ghost, the 37–39

Radcliffe, Betty 25–29
Raynham Hall 7, 15–20, 80
Read, Margaret (Shady Meg) 10–11
Red Cavalier, Raynham Hall 18–20
Red Lady 11
Reeves, Mr and Mrs 48–49
Roberts, Rev Alexander 10
Robertson, Fletcher 106
Roudham Cross 104
Runton 104

Sadler, John 36
St Withburga 34–35
Salthouse 108
Sampson, Charles 33, 87–90
Sandringham 78–80
Scarfe, Baron Rudolph 73
Scole Inn, near Diss 75
Seagrim, Mrs 45–46
Sheffield, Lord 74–75
Sheringham 105
'Shiners' 103
Shipdham 82–83
Shira, Indra 19
Smith, Mary 10
Snettisham 40–46
Squirrel, Mr 50–52
Stalham Broad 87–90
Stiffkey 107
Stone, Lucia 16
Suffling, E.R. 39
Sutton, John 115, 117

Tap and Spile, Norwich 74
Taylor Smith, Peter 109
Thetford 25–29
Thorpe Market 76
Thurlton 102
Timeslips 47–52
Townshend, Marchioness Gwladys 18, 20
Tudor Rose Hotel, King's Lynn 71–72

Walpole, Dorothy 15–16, 80
Walpole, Mary 65–66
Waxham Hall 121–122
Webster, Keith 116–117
Wells-next-the-Sea 107
White Ladies 65–69
Will o' the Wisps 102
Windham, William (III) 91–93
Wolterton Hall 65–66
Woods, Maurice 82
Worstead 67–68, 121–122
Wroxham 30–33
Wroxham Broad 54